Six Sigma in Transactional and Service Environments

Six Sigma in Transactional and Service Environments

HASAN AKPOLAT

GOWER

Published by
Gower Publishing Limited
Gower House
Croft Road
Aldershot
Hants GU11 3HR
England

Gower Publishing Company
Suite 420
101 Cherry Street
Burlington,
VT 05401-4405
USA

Hasan Akpolat has asserted his right under the Copyright, Designs and Patents Act 1988 to be identified as the author of this work.

British Library Cataloguing in Publication Data
Akpolat, Hasan
    Six sigma in transactional and service environments
    1. Customer relations. 2. Customer relations – Case studies
    3. Six sigma (Quality control standard) 4. Service industries
    – Management 5. Service industries – Management – Case
    studies
    I. Title
    658.8'12

ISBN: 0 566 08577 1

Library of Congress Cataloging-in-Publication Data
Akpolat, Hasan.
    Six sigma in transactional and service environments / by Hasan Akpolat.
        p. cm
    Includes index.
    ISBN 0-566-08577-1
    1. Service industries -- Management. 2. Six sigma (Quality control
    standard) 3. Service industries -- Quality control -- Statistical methods. 4. Quality control
    -- Statistical methods. I. Title.
        HD9980.5.A39 2004
        658.4'013--dc22

                                                2004005222

Typeset by Bournemouth Colour Press, Parkstone, Poole.
Printed in Great Britain by MPG Books Ltd, Bodmin.

Contents

List of Figures

Preface

Since its introduction in the 1980s, Six Sigma has gained enormous worldwide popularity, and it appears that it will be around for quite a while. Like many quality improvement initiatives, Six Sigma emerged from the manufacturing environment. In recent years, however, we have witnessed a large number of companies deploying Six Sigma across their organization, including the transactional and service areas of their business, to reduce cost, improve service and stay ahead of competition.

This book is not about the plethora of management theories that abound in business. It is about the practical application of the Six Sigma methodology to transactional and service areas of business. It is the author's wish that this book should contribute to a better understanding of Six Sigma and provide more clarity about its nature and usage, particularly in the transactional and service areas.

Six Sigma is not only appropriate for manufacturing operations but also for service and transactional areas of a business, including:

- purchasing and supply chain
- transport and logistics
- sales and marketing
- facilities and building maintenance
- accounting and finance
- IT services
- human resources, and
- call centres and customer service.

In fact, most of these functions and processes are also used by manufacturing companies. Transactional and service areas of business, however, may differ from manufacturing processes in many ways. One of the typical differences is, for instance, the type of skills and experience required for personnel. Traditionally, an engineer will be more skilled in technical and scientific subjects, including statistics, and the sales or marketing manager will have better understanding of customer and market related issues and accounting. Differences like this have an effect on the application of the Six Sigma tools and techniques, but not on the concept that underlies Six Sigma. In this book, the difference between the manufacturing and non-manufacturing processes have been taken into account by focusing on the implementation of the Six Sigma methodology rather than on the statistical tools and techniques.

In the 1980s, when it was first used by Motorola, Six Sigma had the primary purpose of achieving a drastic reduction in the number of product defects. Motorola coined the term 'Six Sigma' as a desired quality level for its electronic pagers that had no more than 3.4 defects per million parts (or opportunities). This was the original purpose and meaning of

Six Sigma. Today, however, Six Sigma is understood as a robust quality and process improvement concept that is being used by many companies not only to improve the quality of their products and services but also to achieve quantifiable financial results, improve management style and communication and increase customer and employee satisfaction.

As companies differ in size, culture, geographic location and their operations, so too does the implementation of Six Sigma and its deployment. Due to these organizational differences, Six Sigma cannot be copied from one company and applied to another. Six Sigma is a straightforward and user-friendly concept and comprises a number of common elements which can be applied to almost every business; however, special care must be taken with the elements that require customization to suit the organization's needs.

In most organizations, the implementation of Six Sigma generally happens in three fundamentally different phases. *Phase One* is the introduction of Six Sigma to the organization. *Phase Two* is the maturity stage, and *Phase Three* is achieved when Six Sigma becomes part of the company culture. The extent of staff involvement and training, use of statistical tools and the types of projects will be different at each phase of the implementation. Successful implementation of Six Sigma depends largely on how these phases are managed.

This book is a reflection of my own experience as practitioner, consultant and university lecturer in the past 16 years, during which I helped many companies implement Six Sigma both in the manufacturing and non-manufacturing sectors. It has been written for newcomers as well as for experienced practitioners who are interested in improving processes in everyday business operations. The main purpose of this book is to provide the reader with some practical and useful guidelines for Six Sigma deployment and its application to transactional and service processes. It is not about the application of numerous statistical tools and techniques which can be used for process improvement. Although some of the commonly used tools have been introduced and discussed throughout the book, the main emphasis has been placed on both the concept and the implementation of Six Sigma, particularly within the transactional and service areas of business.

This book has two parts. Part One provides the necessary knowledge for understanding of the Six Sigma methodology and its underlying concepts. It has been divided into five main sections, as depicted in Figure P.1; each is described in a separate chapter.

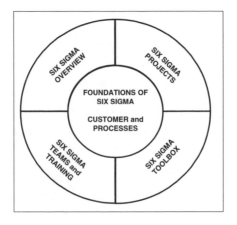

Figure P.1   Six Sigma methodology and its underlying concepts

Part Two consists of practical examples of Six Sigma application to transactional and service environments which have been provided in the form of real-world case studies written by authors from internationally successful companies including Sony, Samsung, Queensland Rail and Malaysia Airlines. These case studies are intended to complement the reader's knowledge of Six Sigma and to increase comprehension of issues surrounding Six Sigma implementations.

In a typical Six Sigma fashion, this book is the result of team effort. It would have not been possible without the valuable contributions of my dear friends and colleagues who provided excellent examples of practical Six Sigma applications to transactional and service environments in the form of case studies. I am grateful for their contributions.

In preparing this book, I have received generous help and advice from numerous people. My special thanks and credit go to my publisher Jonathan Norman and editor Guy Loft for guiding me through the project. I'd like to thank Ms Vanessa Craig from Queensland Rail and Dr David Davis from University of Technology Sydney for reading and commenting on the drafts. I also wish to thank Ms Reiko Tanaka and Mr Albert Lee from Sony Six Sigma Office for their friendship and support over the past few years during my time with Sony Australia. The last word of acknowledgement goes to my friends at IQPC and MarcusEvans for their continuing support at numerous national and international conferences.

Hasan Akpolat

Six Sigma
Methodology

1 *Six Sigma Overview*

Introduction

In recent years, much has been published about Six Sigma in the business and academic press and on the Internet. Despite this fact, there is still confusion among many people, particularly those who work in the transactional and service environments, about the nature of Six Sigma. Two of the fundamental questions often asked are: 'What is Six Sigma?' and 'What is its relevance?' Other questions frequently asked include: 'Is it just a fad like some other management programmes before?' 'Is it only applicable to selected industries and businesses?' 'What are the benefits for my business?' 'How practical is the concept and how easily can it be adapted to my business?' In this chapter, we attempt to provide answers to these and other commonly asked questions not outlined above.

This chapter focuses on what Six Sigma *is* and what it *isn't*. After a brief definition of Six Sigma, it provides a historical context and tracks the benefits of Six Sigma to business from its inception until now. It also provides some guidelines on the use of Six Sigma as a business strategy and how it can be integrated with other management practices to suit the preferences and culture of an organization.

What is Six Sigma?

Simply put, Six Sigma is a business improvement concept that is built upon a well-defined and robust infrastructure which directly involves personnel from several management levels targeting quality and process improvement projects to drive a company's continual improvement efforts.

It is used by many companies not only to improve the quality of their products and services but also to achieve quantifiable financial results, improve management style and communication, and achieve customer and employee satisfaction.

The Six Sigma methodology is a result of the evolutionary process of quality innovations over the past five decades. It combines quality improvement tools with strategic management processes to achieve substantial bottom-line results and improve the overall performance of an organization.

The main characteristics of the Six Sigma methodology include:

- strategic alignment
- top-down approach
- customer focus
- management and staff involvement
- project management
- measurement and improvement.

For some sceptics, Six Sigma is another quality improvement fad primarily used by manufacturing companies. It mainly focuses on defect reduction and as a consequence will soon disappear.

There are two misconceptions inherent in this view. The first is about the nature of the Six Sigma methodology being only suitable to manufacturing, as it traditionally focused on defect reduction and as a result cannot be directly applied to the transactional and service environments. It is true that Six Sigma, like the other quality improvement frameworks ISO 9000 and Total Quality Management (TQM) before it, was used first in the manufacturing environments. However, many corporations, including General Electric and Sony, have successfully applied Six Sigma to their transactional and service processes as well and achieved substantial financial benefits.

The second misconception that Six Sigma will soon disappear is countered by the fact it has been almost two decades since Six Sigma was launched by Motorola and is presently preferred by many organizations as the best methodology to drive their quality and process improvement initiatives.

In the 1980s, when Six Sigma was launched, larger manufacturing companies were already using quality improvement programmes or models such as the ISO 9000 standards or TQM. However, in the early 1990s, many of these organizations started to realize that ISO 9000 or TQM initiatives did not achieve the expected process improvements across the company or provide substantial financial savings. Thus, many companies looked for a more flexible and robust programme, which led to Six Sigma.

Within this context, the electronics giant Sony is an interesting study. Sony enjoys a worldwide reputation for the excellence of its products. So, what was the reason for Sony deploying Six Sigma across its entire corporation and what were the characteristics of its Six Sigma implementation programme? According to the CEO, Mr Nobuyuki Idei, Sony was undergoing a fundamental change in its operations that would transform Sony from an electronics manufacturer into a 'personal broadband network solution' company. This effectively meant that Sony was determined to combine its already strong electronics business (hardware) with personalized solutions (content) and make them available to consumers via the Internet so that they can be accessed wherever and whenever needed. To achieve this corporate strategic goal, Sony used three core strategic initiatives:

- Value Creation Management
- Supply Chain Management and
- Sony Six Sigma.

Although generally adopted from General Electric's implementation, Sony has customized Six Sigma to suit to its corporate direction and company culture. For Sony, the main purpose of its customized Six Sigma model was not only to further improve product quality but also to improve management quality. By using the Sony Six Sigma (SSS) methodology, Sony managers learned how to lower risk when making decisions and to reduce costs in daily operations. According to Mr Idei, Sony Six Sigma enabled the company to realize more than 30 billion yen in financial benefits within the first three years of its implementation. Like many other larger companies, Sony is implementing Six Sigma not only in its manufacturing plants but also in the transactional and service processes. A corporate memorandum was distributed to all Sony operations around the globe to highlight the importance of the implementation of Sony Six Sigma (see Figure 1.1).

Dear Sirs,

Re: In Developing Business Plans for the Fiscal Year 2001

With the completion of mid-term plan for the fiscal year 2000, I trust that each network company will begin developing their business plans for the fiscal year 2001. In doing so, I would like to ask that you keep the following points in mind, in accordance with the Sony Six Sigma approach.

1.   Incorporate Sony Six Sigma in setting business plan targets.

2.   Clearly define who your customers are. Incorporate their 'voice' (VOC = voice of customer) in your business plan.

3.   Set ambitious targets with making a breakthrough in mind. In doing so, do not depend on your intuition, but make sure to benchmark others.

4.   Use appropriate evaluation metrics to ensure that progress is being made toward achieving the target.

5.   Use both the 'CE Diagram (cause and effect diagram)' and 'CTQ Diagram (critical to quality diagram)' employed by Sony Six Sigma Champions, in addition to the business plan format that is supplied to you by headquarters. Submit your diagrams together with your business plan.

Yours sincerely
Kunitake Ando
President and COO
Sony Corporation

Figure 1.1   Six Sigma implementation as a corporate directive

Six Sigma is a long-term initiative although it has been proved by many organizations that it can also generate immediate improvements in profitability and the bottom line. In contrast to other quality improvement methodologies used in the past, Six Sigma provides a very well-defined specification for how to train and involve staff from several management levels (a top-down approach), how to carry out the improvement projects, and how to use statistical tools and techniques for process improvement.

The Sony experience showed that Six Sigma can be customized by any organization to suit its cultural and strategic preferences, without loss of its essential robustness, and deliver substantial financial benefits.

The advent of Six Sigma

As mentioned in the previous section, Six Sigma is a result of the evolutionary process of quality innovations. During 50 years in the history of quality, there were various milestones which shaped the modern view of quality (Figure 1.2). The first real quality innovation was the use of statistics in manufacturing processes. The use of tools such as control charts goes

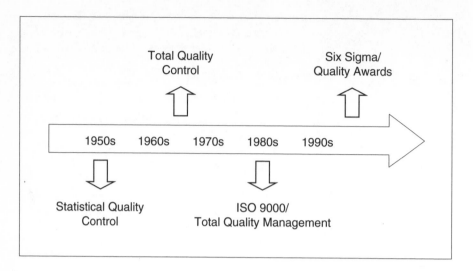

Figure 1.2   The evolution of quality innovations

back to the 1930s. However, quality became an important strategic element during World War II when the US military started to use military standards as a means of assuring the quality of its critical machinery and weapons systems, particularly those manufactured by numerous subcontractors. After World War II, as part of the reconstruction process of its economy, Japan adopted many of the American statistical quality control techniques and blended them with Japanese thought, culture and tradition to create a new quality concept called 'Total Quality Control' (TQC).

In the 1960s and 1970s, the TQC methodology proved to be an effective way of producing high quality and reliable products, which helped Japanese companies gain impressive market share in some industries, including electronics, automobiles and shipbuilding. In the 1980s, Western companies responded to the Japanese challenge with two parallel developments: the ISO 9000 quality assurance system model predominantly favoured by the European Union and the adoption of the Japanese TQC concept under the banner of Total Quality Management.

Both ISO 9000 and TQM assisted many organizations in improving product and service quality. However, at the same time many companies recognized that ISO 9000 and TQM were inadequate in improving processes further and achieving substantial bottom-line results. It is the author's view that the current quality era can be defined by two significantly different, but parallel, developments: Six Sigma and Quality Awards. In fact, Motorola was not only the first company applying Six Sigma but also was among the recipients of the first American Quality Award in 1988. A Quality Award model (in some countries referred to as 'the Business Excellence Framework') is usually applied as a framework for organizational development, while Six Sigma is typically used as a method of improving processes and achieving better financial results.

As one of the latest quality improvement innovations of the last century, Six Sigma was the result of an evolutionary process. Some of the tools and techniques used in Six Sigma are not new and were developed in the last 50 years. Since its inception in the 1980s, Six Sigma has developed remarkably and is increasingly gaining international popularity in Europe and Asia as well.

There are three major stages of Six Sigma development to date (see Figure 1.3). In the late 1980s and early 1990s, Six Sigma was used mainly by US American multinationals and predominantly in the manufacturing environment to reduce product defects and improve productivity. In the late 1990s, Six Sigma gained enormous acceptance mainly due to the successful and spectacular application led by Jack Welch, former chairman and CEO of General Electric. In the past few years, not only has the number of international Six Sigma applications increased, but it has been also applied to almost every business function including research and development, customer service, accounts payable, human resources and IT services.

Benefits of Six Sigma

There are several reasons why organizations adopt and implement Six Sigma. They include:

- a desire to reduce cost and waste
- a desire to improve productivity
- the need to transform the organization
- a response to competitive pressure
- benchmarking with other market leaders
- pressure from customers to improve the quality of products and services
- the wish to drive a new corporate direction.

Whatever the specific reason, most companies today are operating in a business environment which has the following characteristics:

- accelerating technology
- a globalizing market

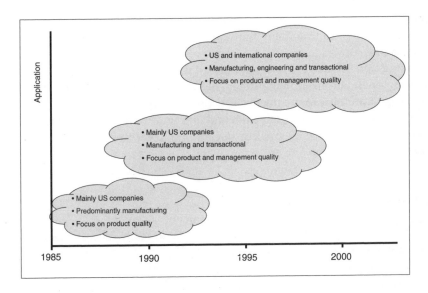

Figure 1.3   The evolution of Six Sigma

- fierce competition and
- sophisticated, more demanding customers.

In the late twentieth century, we have witnessed enormous changes imposed by information and communication technologies such as the Internet. Not only the way businesses operate but also everything we as individuals do – how we learn, how we communicate and how we live – is changing exponentially. We have entered the 'Information Age', also referred to as the 'Knowledge Age'. This and other challenges, such as the market globalization, are forcing organizations to rethink their entire business directions, structures and operations as part of their survival strategy. As a result of market globalization and increased competition, for instance, organizations are constantly looking for better ways to maximize profit. Outsourcing operations to low-cost countries seems to be a common practice for many organizations. Not only manufacturing but also transactional and service processes are under scrutiny. Setting up call centres in low-cost regions was a common trend in the 1990s. Some companies are now outsourcing the entire accounts-payable operations and other transactional areas of their business to low-cost countries because:

(a) the cost of operations is much lower in those countries, and
(b) the technology enables them to do so.

In such an environment of rapid changes, companies are increasingly demanding a robust methodology that can assist them in keeping up with the competition. What they need is increased process efficiency, cost reduction and improved bottom-line results. For many companies, Six Sigma has been able to deliver those results.

The real power of Six Sigma comes from its top-down management approach. If used correctly, Six Sigma is an extremely powerful concept for driving a company-wide continuous improvement programme. As with any management initiative, Six Sigma is dependent on top management commitment and involvement. However, unlike the other improvement programmes, top management plays a clearly defined role within Six Sigma. Not only do they have to lead the initiative, but they also have to be actively involved in the Six Sigma projects.

One of the main benefits of Six Sigma is that it improves communication among various management levels. All Six Sigma participants have to undergo a well-defined training programme and learn how to use the quality improvement tools effectively. Six Sigma tools have clearly defined application guidelines and link improvement efforts to organizational goals and objectives. Using these tools throughout the company enables managers literally to speak the 'same' language.

Six Sigma as a core strategy

As highlighted in the case studies in Part II of this book, many organizations are using Six Sigma to achieve strategic business goals including:

- managing the culture change within an organization
- challenging the competition with new ideas and innovation

- forming and improving supplier–customer relations
- expanding businesses into foreign and domestic markets
- transforming business structures and/or operations.

Six Sigma methodology and its various tools can be used for multiple purposes, including process improvement (problem-solving), developing and mapping strategic goals, and staff development. For instance, the cause-and-effect (CE) diagram is typically used as a problem-solving tool. However, the CE diagram also identifies the actions needed to achieve a goal. As shown in Figure 1.4, the CE diagram, sometimes referred to as the Fishbone diagram or Ishikawa diagram, has been used for this purpose. The tail reflects the current state of business and the head indicates the target or the goal set. The bones branching from the spine contain those things that need to be implemented in order to achieve the target. It is a simple but very effective graphic (business) planning tool.

Sony, for instance, uses the CE diagram to cascade down its corporate goals and objectives to process levels (Figure 1.5). The CE diagram is used by the various Sony companies:

- to coordinate and communicate their joint improvement efforts
- for business planning and reporting and
- as part of the management performance evaluation system.

Another very useful graphic Six Sigma tool is the tree diagram. It can be used for many purposes. One of its useful applications is to break down an objective and identify the actions required to achieve that objective. The top part in the Figure 1.6 illustrates a generic use of this simple diagram to align Six Sigma projects with organizational goals and objectives. The bottom part in the same figure illustrates the use of the tree diagram to align Sony Six Sigma projects with corporate vision and organizational goals.

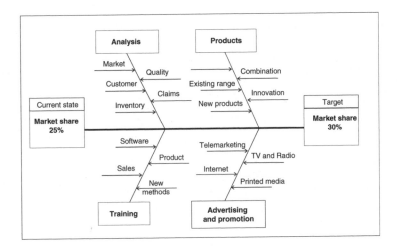

Figure 1.4   Cause-and-effect chart used as a planning tool

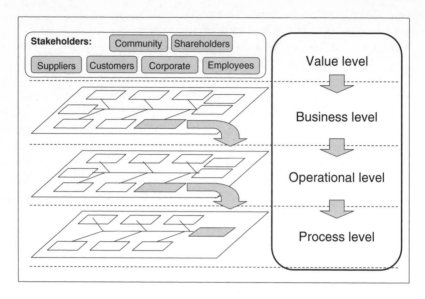

Figure 1.5   Use of the CE chart to cascade down a plan or goal from business level to process level

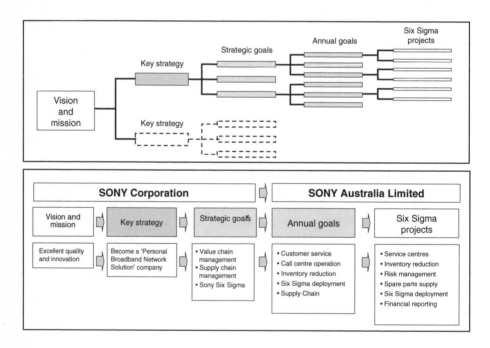

Figure 1.6   Aligning Six Sigma with organizational goals and objectives

Measuring Six Sigma

The symbol sigma (σ) is the nineteenth letter of the Greek alphabet, in lower case, and is commonly used for expressing the standard deviation of a normal distribution which is represented by a bell-shaped curve. With increasing numerical values for sigma the bell-shaped curve becomes flatter, meaning that observations are getting further away from the centre of the distribution. In other words, a higher numerical value for sigma means a higher spread of the data (curve) as shown in Figure 1.7. As spread is typically used as a measure of variation within a process, the main idea behind process improvement is for it to reduce the variation and therefore the spread of the data. The primary objective is to minimize process variation to an optimum (economically practical) level.

Using the standard deviation, we can also identify how many observations would fall within the sigma limits. For instance, in a normally distributed data, ±1σ (a distance between one sigma to the left and one sigma to the right from the average) means that 68 per cent of all observations would fall within those limits and 32 per cent of data is outside of the ±1σ limits. As illustrated in Figure 1.8, the number of observations falling outside of the curve decreases with increasing sigma.

Let's apply this to a transactional process. If we imagine that a bank has 1 000 000 transactions per month and the process is at three sigma level, 2700 out of 1 000 000 of those transactions would be outside the three-sigma limits (first and second columns in Figure 1.9). Improving the same process to six sigma (six times sigma) would mean that only 2 out of 1 billion transactions would be outside of those limits. A process at six sigma level would mean a state of near perfection. Most processes in transactional and service environments typically operate below three-sigma levels, unless it is a process which has specific legislative requirements (for instance, safety or environmental regulations) or is running at higher financial risks. The identification of the sigma level required for a process depends on various factors including customer and market pressures, resource availability and other strategic decisions.

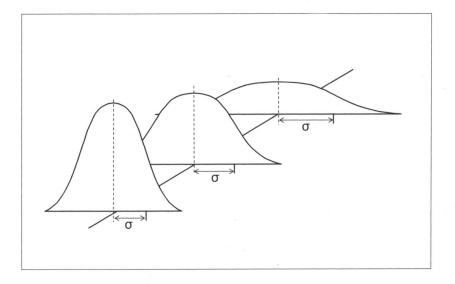

Figure 1.7   Use of standard deviation (σ) as a measure of spread of data

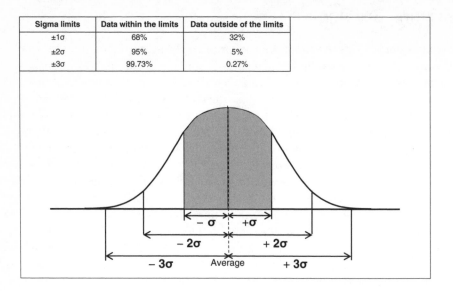

Sigma limits	Data within the limits	Data outside of the limits
±1σ	68%	32%
±2σ	95%	5%
±3σ	99.73%	0.27%

Figure 1.8   Sigma limits and corresponding data percentages within and outside of those limits

Sigma level	Number of defects per million opportunities (DPMO)	
	Process centred (Short term situation)	Process shifted by 1.5 σ (Long term situation)
1 σ	317 400	697 700
2 σ	45 400	308 537
3 σ	2700	66 807
4 σ	63	6210
5 σ	0.57	233
6 σ	0.002	3.4

Figure 1.9   Sigma levels and corresponding number of defects per million opportunities

The interpretation that Six Sigma equals to two defects out of 1 billion transactions was based on the assumption that the process mean is centred. After studying extensive empirical data, Motorola engineers determined that most processes shift over time as much as 1.5σ from the desired process average. In Figure 1.9, the third column illustrates this effect. The long-term situation is referred to as the 'process sigma level', while the short-term situation is called the 'statistical sigma level'.

Integrating Six Sigma with other management practices

This section looks at the integration of Six Sigma with the following quality improvement programmes:

- ISO 9000 quality system

- Business Process Management (BPM)
- Total Quality Management (TQM) and
- Business Excellence Frameworks.

ISO 9000 QUALITY SYSTEM

In the 1980s, to a certain extent as a response by the Western world to the Japanese industrial challenges, two major approaches emerged in the quality area: the ISO 9000 quality system and the TQM philosophies. The ISO 9000 gained enormous popularity in the late 1990s due to the Conformity Assessment Model used by the European Union. This model gave privileges to companies who had a certified ISO 9000 quality system in place. As a result, many countries within the EU and those supplying products and services to the EU implemented the ISO 9000 system predominantly as means of compliance with the ISO 9000 quality standards, which allowed them to obtain entry into EU countries.

It is argued by many quality practitioners that compliance with the ISO 9000 standards does not achieve better quality products and services. Previous ISO 9000 standards (1994 version) required organizations to implement written procedures in the areas identified by the standards (the 'famous' 20 elements). This requirement has now been dropped in the new ISO 9000 standards (2000 version), recognizing the fact that documenting a process alone does not necessarily improve the process. As a result, the 2000 version of ISO 9000 is now believed to be more flexible and compatible with other quality improvement frameworks. In the centre of the new ISO 9000 standards is the so-called 'continual improvement model' (see Figure 1.10). It seems that the standards have been specifically modified to become closer to the Business Excellence Frameworks.

The first impression one gets from the model is that it illustrates the well-known Shewhart Wheel's (sometimes referred to as the Deming Cycle) 'Plan-Do-Check-Act' in the anticlockwise direction, 'resource management' being 'Plan', 'product realization' being 'Do'

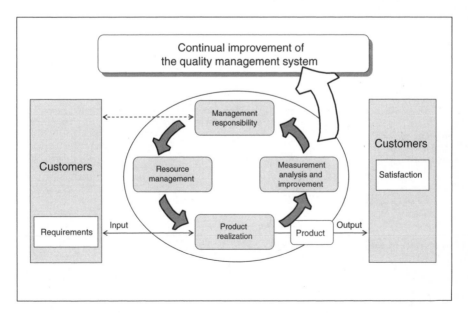

Figure 1.10   The ISO 9000 continual improvement model

and so on. The new ISO 9000 standards also use a set of 'quality principles' to complement this model. The quality principles include:

- leadership
- customer focus
- process approach
- system approach
- factual approach
- supplier relationships
- involvement of people
- continual improvement.

A closer look at the quality principle 'process approach' can assist in understanding the underlying concept behind the new ISO standard. The process approach can be demonstrated by the three main activities:

- identifying the core processes
- determining the key performance indicators (KPIs) and
- monitoring the processes.

This approach recognizes the fact that organizations are different and so are the processes they employ. The new ISO 9000 now requires companies to identify their core processes and determine their metrics (KPIs), in order to monitor and improve them. But it does not describe how this should be done. It is argued by many quality practitioners that it is not the purpose of the ISO 9000 standards to prescribe any specific programme or initiative to be used for process improvement. Six Sigma is perfectly suitable for this purpose.

A simplified model as shown in Figure 1.11 can be used to meet the process approach

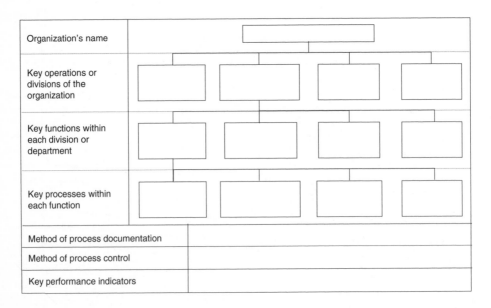

Figure 1.11 A simplified model of compliance with the ISO 9000 process approach requirements

requirements of the ISO 9000 standard. This model is also used as source of process information when carrying out a Six Sigma project. Identification of the key divisions, key functions and key processes can be performed readily by using organizational charts and other human resources documents such as positions descriptions. These days, most companies maintain their documentation systems online in electronic format, so this information is usually readily available. Other documentation sources may include product manuals, photographs, drawings, etc.

The method of process control in transactional (or service) processes differs slightly from manufacturing. In manufacturing, process control is usually performed by using a device to obtain information about the quality characteristics of a product and comparing this result (measurement) with the specification values. One of the commonly used process control methods in the transactional and service environments is the review of the process data collected over a specified period of time. These reviews are often performed by an individual (manager) or a team of specialists to identify corrective actions.

Figure 1.12 illustrates the application of the process approach model to transactional processes. In this example, 'procurement and inventory' has been identified as one of the core processes within the Sony Australia's administration and operations department which in turn forms one of the key functions of the AV-IT products division. In this example, process documentation was maintained in the business application system (SAP) and in the departmental website of the company intranet. The administration and operations department implemented weekly supply chain meetings and monthly procurement meetings as the means of applying process controls at which inventory levels, product freshness and timely supply are checked against requirements and corrective actions are identified where necessary.

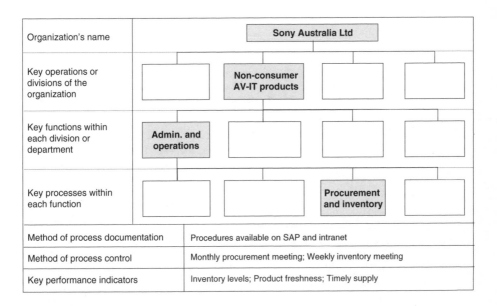

Figure 1.12 Application of the process approach model to transactional processes

BUSINESS PROCESS MANAGEMENT

One of the commonly used and simple definitions of Business Process Management (BPM) is that it is a concept used to better manage and improve business processes. There are numerous models currently used by various organizations. Most of the BPM models consist of several aspects including the human aspect, the information aspect, and the process aspect. In this book, a simplified model is used to discuss the process aspect of the BPM approach, its main characteristics and how it can be integrated with Six Sigma.

As illustrated in Figure 1.13, the main characteristics of the simplified BPM model include:

- process leadership
- process documentation
- process control and
- process improvement.

A sound BPM system starts with the identification of the key processes and the personnel who are responsible for these processes. 'Responsibility' in this context means the 'process leadership', which includes the process ownership and process awareness. It is quite common in the transactional and service environments for many people to be unaware of the owner of the processes and how they actually perform. Identifying process owners is also one of the critical requirements of the Six Sigma methodology. Within Six Sigma, process ownership and current process status must be determined before selecting any Six Sigma projects.

Once process leadership (ownership) issues have been identified and addressed, the next step is to map the process. In most cases, this can be done using existing quality system documentation or any other process documentation sources. Process documentation can be in paper or electronic form.

Process control requires the collection and analysis of process data. Within Six Sigma,

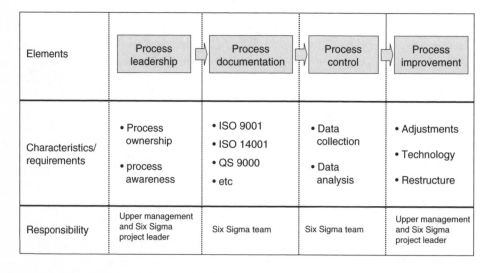

Elements	Process leadership	Process documentation	Process control	Process improvement
Characteristics/ requirements	• Process ownership • process awareness	• ISO 9001 • ISO 14001 • QS 9000 • etc	• Data collection • Data analysis	• Adjustments • Technology • Restructure
Responsibility	Upper management and Six Sigma project leader	Six Sigma team	Six Sigma team	Upper management and Six Sigma project leader

Figure 1.13   Characteristics of a simplified BPM model and its integration with Six Sigma

the activities 'process documentation' and 'process control' are typically performed by the Six Sigma project teams. Process improvement is perhaps the most important element of the process management approach as it involves collective decision making by upper management and Six Sigma project leaders. In some cases, adjustments to processes or the implementation of new technologies (for instance purchasing new hardware or a new version of a software application) will result in the desired improvement. In other cases, it might be necessary to restructure the process by outsourcing or amalgamating with an existing process.

TOTAL QUALITY MANAGEMENT

Total Quality Management (TQM) was the second major development within the quality movement in the 1980s. TQM started in the manufacturing sectors (automotive and electronics industries) first and then spread to the transactional and service environments in the 1990s. Simply put, TQM can be described as a management philosophy which focuses on customers and involves employees from all departments of an organization to continually improve the quality of products and services. 'Continuous improvement' (CI) was the main concept behind the TQM philosophy. To do this, employees were trained to be part of the TQM teams. Most organizations used two different types of TQM teams: the Quality Council and the Quality Circle.

Both teams were permanent teams and consisted of several employees. The Quality Council was a cross-functional team which mainly consisted of members of middle management and was tasked to drive the TQM initiative. Quality Circle was a group of six to eight people selected from departmental staff and tasked with solving quality problems within their own work area.

In many organizations TQM contributed to better understanding of customer requirements, improving staff morale and solving quality problems. Many critics, however, felt TQM eventually failed due to lack of direction and structured approach from upper management.

Six Sigma takes the idea of CI to a higher level. It provides a robust methodology through its well-defined team structures, strategic alignment and top-down approach. Six Sigma teams are vertical teams involving management from at least three different levels of the organizational hierarchy (Figure 1.14). Another important characteristic of the Six Sigma team structure is that, unlike the TQM teams, they are non-permanent teams. They are formed to carry out an improvement project with a clearly defined objective, scope and time frame. After the achievement of project goals, teams decease in order to be re-formed according to the requirements of another improvement project.

In many organizations, Six Sigma teams replaced the Quality Councils. However, it is the author's belief that there is still need for Quality Circles as they can run side by side with Six Sigma teams. In fact, many organizations implementing Six Sigma assign smaller and less complex Six Sigma projects to the Quality Circles.

BUSINESS EXCELLENCE FRAMEWORKS

The term 'business excellence' refers basically to an organization which is recognized for its performance in delivering excellent business results, for instance in innovativeness, business improvement and long term success. The Business Excellence Framework (in some countries

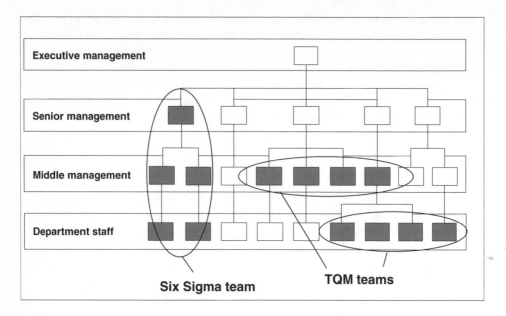

Figure 1.14   Comparison of Six Sigma and TQM teams

referred to as the 'Quality Award') is a model that is used to define a set of criteria for organizational self-assessment and the basis for judging entrants to a national or international award scheme.

The Quality Award models are used in almost every industrialized country as a framework for achieving best-in-class results for organizational performance. Some of the more popular Quality Award schemes include:

- the Malcolm Baldrige National Quality Award (MBNQA) in the USA
- the European Foundation for Quality Management (EFQM) Excellence Model
- the Deming Prize in Japan and
- the Australian Business Excellence Framework (ABEF).

All Quality Award models typically use a set of criteria for assessment. The ABEF, for instance, has seven performance categories:

1. Leadership and Innovation
2. Strategy and Planning Processes
3. Data, Information and Knowledge
4. People
5. Customer and Market Focus
6. Processes, Products and Services
7. Business Results.

Each assessment category consists of several performance items. The sixth category (Processes, Products and Services), for instance, consists of the following items:

6.1   Innovation process
6.2   Supplier and partner processes
6.3   Management and improvement of processes
6.4   Quality of products and services.

Each performance item is evaluated by using a model called 'Approach-Deploy-Review-Improvement' (ADRI):

- 'Approach' refers to plans and structures being utilized by the organization
- 'Deploy' refers to the way that those plans and structures are used
- 'Review' includes measurement and analysis of the outcomes
- 'Improvement' refers to the way that the organization learns from its experience.

If used correctly, Business Excellence Frameworks can generate substantial benefits to organizations, including better leadership, increased customer and employee satisfaction, improved processes and better financial results. They typically describe the overall framework for improvement but do not recommend or prescribe any specific programme or methodology to be used. As discussed earlier in conjunction with the ISO 9000 quality standard, Six Sigma provides the concept for improvement and can be easily integrated with Business Excellence. In fact, in many organizations, Business Excellence and Six Sigma are used together; Business Excellence provides the overall framework and direction for management while Six Sigma is deployed as an improvement methodology.

Summary

Six Sigma methodology can be categorized into characteristics and their corresponding aspects, as shown in Figure 1.15.
   The characteristics 'strategic alignment' and 'top-down approach' form the management aspect of the Six Sigma methodology which has been discussed in this chapter. 'Customer focus' and 'measurement and improvement' form the foundation of Six Sigma and will be discussed in detail in Chapter 2. The characteristic 'management and staff involvement' refers to the Six Sigma infrastructure aspect and will be covered in Chapter 4. 'Project management' refers to the method through which Six Sigma improvements are achieved

Characteristics	Aspect	Discussed in Chapter
Customer focus	Customer	2
Strategic alignment	Management	1
Top-down approach	Management	1
Management and staff involvement	Infrastructure	4
Project management	Method	3
Measurement and improvement	Process	2

Figure 1.15   Characteristics of Six Sigma

and will be discussed in Chapter 3. In addition, the method of constructing some basic tools and charts will be covered in Chapter 5.

The name 'Six Sigma' is derived from the use of standard deviation as a measure of defect levels in manufacturing processes. Using the Motorola definition, a process operating at six-sigma level (six times sigma) would mean less than four defects per million opportunities, a level close to perfection.

The Six Sigma methodology is a result of the evolutionary process of quality innovations from the 1930s through TQC, ISO 9000 and TQM. It is a business concept that combines quality improvement tools with strategic management processes to drive a company's continual improvement efforts and achieve substantial bottom-line results.

The strength of Six Sigma lies in the fact that:

- it is truly an open management technology and is not managed or owned by anyone
- it can be easily customized by any implementing organization to suit various management goals
- it is not merely focused on defect reduction but can be applied to all areas of business including transactional and service environments
- it is supported by a well-defined toolbox for measurement and analysing processes employed
- it creates a platform for internal and external communication where experiences and knowledge can be shared.

Many organizations use Six Sigma not as a stand-alone system but integrated with other management practices, such as the ISO 9000 quality system, BPM, TQM or Business Excellence, as they complement each other.

2 *Foundations of Six Sigma: Customer and Processes*

Introduction

No organization can survive without customers. Together with process, customers are considered to be the foundation of Six Sigma. It is necessary to identify who they are, what they need and what processes are required to satisfy those needs. Six Sigma recognizes the duality of customer and process and provides the mechanisms for ensuring that this relationship is established, maintained and strengthened.

In this chapter we first explore who the customers are, what they expect and how to measure their needs and their satisfaction. Process thinking as the underlying concept of Six Sigma is discussed by first exploring processes as an abstraction and then providing answers to fundamental questions such as how to define processes and how to map, measure and improve them.

Although customers and processes are treated in a generic fashion by this chapter, nonetheless the principal focus is on how customers and processes relate to the transactional and service environments.

Understanding the customers

Whether manufacturing or non-manufacturing, all organizations have customers and most companies provide a combination of products and services to their customers. Understanding and meeting customer expectations is paramount to business success. The term 'customer' usually includes the 'internal' customers and 'external' customers. External customers can be further subdivided into two groups: 'intermediate customers' and 'final customers'.

Internal customers are entities within an organization. Every employee could be a customer or a supplier, depending on whether they receive or provide an output. Intermediate customers can be, for instance, distributors, dealers or franchisees who provide your products or services to final customers. Final customers are entities who receive or consume goods and services at the end of the supply chain, and are often referred to as the 'end users' or 'after-sales customers'. Intermediate or final customers could include prospective or potential customers who are interested in an organization's goods and services. They are often referred to as the 'before-sales customers'. Throughout this book, the focus is placed on both the internal and external customers, as identified above.

When identifying customers it is important to find out which customers are key customers. The 80/20 rule is commonly used as a starting point for identifying primary customers; for instance, 20 per cent of customers contribute to 80 per cent of company's sales. However, the 80/20 rule rapidly becomes simplistic because it focuses on a single factor only. It does not provide more detailed information on customers. The strategic importance of each customer can only be determined by using a more detailed approach. Some of the factors which have to be considered include:

- the history of the relationship
- market and technology trends
- group characteristics (age, profession, salary, demographics, and so on).

Identifying the customers correctly and meeting their requirements can be crucial for business. A good example of correctly identifying the customer is the Scandinavian Airlines (SAS) experience under Jan Carlzon, the former president of SAS. Carlzon transformed the 'troubled' commercial airline into a successful and service-focused organization within just a few years achieving praise from all corners of the business world. In 1981, SAS identified the frequent business traveller as the key customer group and formed a business strategy around this group. The top management then identified all actions necessary to meet the requirements of this key customer group. Carlzon states in his famous book entitled *Moments of Truth*

> … we scrutinised every resource, every expense, every procedure and asked ourselves, 'Do we need this in order to serve the frequent business traveller?' If the answer was no, then we were prepared to phase out the expense or procedure, no matter what it was or how dear it was to those within the company. If the answer was yes, then we were prepared to spend more money to develop it further and make SAS more competitive … .[1]

Ignorance of customer needs can be very costly, sometimes leading to organizational disasters. A few years ago, I worked with a small telecommunications device manufacturer that was not able to manage the quality of its products, which was of major concern to its key customers. Within only a few years, the company lost its entire business and finally closed its doors. Customers take their business elsewhere if their voice is not heard.

The customers determine the level of quality, not the managers. One of the methods of measuring the level of quality required by customers is the customer survey. Customer surveys often measure customer perceptions rather than quality-related facts; but customer perceptions are just as valid as the reality of numbers of product faults, because customer perception is the customer's reality.

The voice of the customer

It is advisable to identify and understand different types of customer requirements before capturing the 'voice of the customer' (VOC). One of the commonly used tools for visualizing different types of customer requirements is the Kano analysis.

The Kano analysis (Figure 2.1) differentiates between three different types of customer

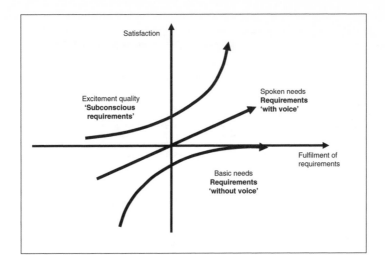

Figure 2.1   The Kano analysis of customer needs

requirements and illustrates how customer satisfaction is linked to these requirements. Basic customer needs are the requirements 'without voice'. They are expected to be there (they are regarded as the 'musts'). Spoken customer needs are the requirements 'with voice'. Customers specifically asked for them (they are regarded as the 'wants'). The subconscious requirements are those requirements that customers did not think of, or did not think would be available or would form a part of the deal. They generate customer excitement if they are or become a part of the deal or are offered for a small additional charge (they are regarded as the 'nice-to-haves').

If the Kano analysis is applied to a restaurant, customers' spoken requirements could be reflected in their selection of a meal from the menu which contains the specification of the meal chosen. The degree of customer satisfaction would largely depend on whether the meal was prepared in the same way as specified in the menu. However, customers also expect some degree of hygiene as a 'basic' requirement. A clean wine glass or cutlery usually does not lead to satisfaction. It will result in dissatisfaction if the hygiene standards are not met. One example of the subconscious requirements would be if the meal was served by a friendly person, who paid special attention to the customer's needs without undue intrusiveness.

The voice-of-the-customer (VOC) chart is a useful depiction tool to summarize the results of the Kano analysis (Figure 2.2). It is a simple Six Sigma tool and typically used to identify the customer requirements. Customer orders and specifications are typical examples of spoken customer needs or requirements 'with voice'. Unspoken or basic needs (requirements 'without voice') help identify areas of dissatisfaction and thus can be used as a method of managing the risk of failure, while addressing the 'subconscious requirements' creates the potential for developing a loyalty relationship with the customer. For further examples of the use of the VOC chart, see also the Sony Australia case study in Part II of this book.

Customer satisfaction is one of the hot topics in business circles. Increased publications in the business media and the fact that many quality awards, such as the Malcolm Baldrige National Quality Award (MBNQA), the Australian Business Excellence Framework (ABEF)

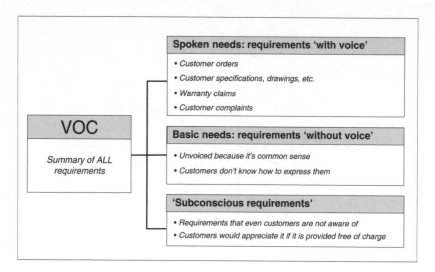

Figure 2.2   The voice-of-the-customer chart

and the European EFQM, have all made customer satisfaction one of their assessment criteria, recognize this. Organizations that have a good understanding of their customers' needs are better able to satisfy them.

Exploring customer needs: The customer survey process

Customer surveys are one of the most commonly used instruments in the transactional and service environments to identify customer needs and measure their satisfaction. Customer surveys are also used by manufacturing companies to understand and assess the perceptions and attitudes of their customers. Understanding customer needs correctly means being able to evaluate and change company direction as appropriate.

The following sources and methods may be used for identification of customer requirements:

- customer interviews
- customer survey questionnaires
- customer visits
- focus groups
- mystery shoppers/callers
- market trend analysis
- warranty claims
- customer complaints
- benchmarking.

CUSTOMER INTERVIEWS

Customer interviews are usually conducted face-to-face or on the phone and often deliver quicker results than other methods. Face-to-face interviews can be time consuming but are powerful methods for identifying qualitative data. When conducting customer interviews, it is necessary that interviews are well prepared in advance. Things to consider include:

- the purpose, duration and location of the interview
- a list of meaningful interview questions
- the details of the people to be interviewed
- the roles of the interviewers during the interview
- expected outcomes of the interview.

CUSTOMER SURVEY QUESTIONNAIRES

Customer survey questionnaires contain a defined set of questions that are designed to capture customers' views and perceptions on goods and services a company is providing and the responses help to understand the customers' changing behaviours. Questionnaires can be used for almost any purpose, and sometimes they can be quite comprehensive, but they do not capture everything. Customer surveys questionnaires can be conducted for identifying customer requirements and measuring customer satisfaction. Figure 2.3 illustrates a typical customer survey process flow with five simple steps.

Step 1: Define goals and objectives of the survey

Many people start developing survey questions before clearly defining goals and objectives of the survey. Goals don't have to be long or complex. One of the good ways of defining goals is to write down what the intention of the survey is. Do you want to find out what your customers think about your company's services? Or do you want to measure what

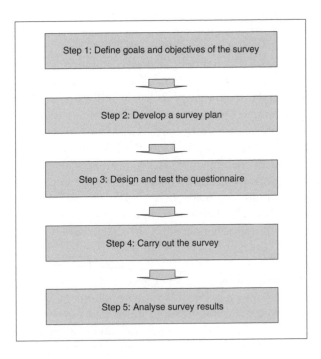

Figure 2.3   Customer survey process flow

employees think about management? Defining goals and objectives of the survey clearly will highlight the important issues and help you stay on track.

Step 2: Develop a survey plan

During the survey-planning phase, a decision should be made on which method is more suitable for the implementation of the survey. Mail or online surveys are usually less expensive than phone surveys if the sample size is large. However, surveys conducted on the phone are quicker in delivering results. It is recommended to prepare a list of criteria for selecting the most suitable method, which may include the implementation cost, sample size, desired response rate, length and complexity of questions, anonymity or confidentiality and time limitations.

Conducting a survey is a typical project management activity that requires a sound project plan. Some of the project plan's key elements include:

- the scope of the survey
- the method of sampling
- resource requirements
- a survey cost analysis
- a survey time plan
- a risk analysis.

Step 3: Design and test the survey questionnaire

The next step is to translate goals and objectives into survey questions. Keep the questionnaire short and simple. Nowadays, people are frequently asked by many organizations to complete questionnaires. Most people feel that filling out long and complex questions is boring and useless, as they see no value in answering those questions. It is particularly frustrating if respondents do not receive feedback on the questionnaires they have filled out. Simple and short questions that have been carefully selected by subject matter experts will increase the chance of achieving a desired response rate.

There are many traps for the novice in designing a survey questionnaire. Customer survey questionnaire design is a science in itself, and most large companies use market research consultancies, universities or survey statisticians to design their surveys, and often to administer them. They can be a costly exercise. The quality of information extracted, and therefore its usability, is very dependent on the soundness of the design. Most survey questionnaires are usually designed based on previous outcomes of other qualitative interviews. During the interviews a full exploration of what might be the most appropriate questions to include should take place. It is possible for sophisticated survey research to identify the underlying drivers of customer preferences and behaviours, and these change over time; therefore, the survey questionnaire design needs to be reviewed between periodically conducted surveys.

Once the questions have been developed, a scale for measurement of respondents' answers must be designed. Choosing the right scale for your survey is an important decision. There is no one scale to suit every need. How many points needed on a scale will depend on how the data will be used. Commonly used scales have three to ten points on them. Two or three points are usually considered as being not sufficiently discriminative. A scale with nine or ten points would raise the concern that, due to the larger scale width, the respondents might not be careful enough when completing the questionnaires. There should always be a word descriptor for each number on the scale, to guide respondents in interpreting how to allocate each number, as shown in Figure 2.4.

Testing the validity of the questionnaire is the next step, which can be performed in many ways. A questionnaire is an instrument (like a measurement device in the manufacturing environment) that can be used to collect data from people and for a number of reasons. Every instrument needs to be calibrated and validated to ensure that what is measured is accurate. 'Validity' means we are satisfied with the instrument and that it measures what it is supposed to measure. In the case of a survey, we can validate the questionnaire by testing it with someone or some group who are not part of the survey team, before sending it out to the actual respondents.

Step 4: Carry out the survey

Surveying your customers can be performed in many ways. Some of the commonly used methods are the mail survey or electronic survey (online survey). Lack of customer motivation for participation is one of the flaws attached to this survey method. That is why many companies offer some incentives to their customers to ensure that a sufficient sample size is obtained from the campaign. Even if a sufficient sample size has been achieved, it could mean data have been obtained only from a specific group rather than randomly, which is the desired objective. Another approach is to combine the survey and interview approach and administer a structured survey in a face-to-face situation, collecting both qualitative and quantitative information.

Step 5: Analysing the survey results

Analysing survey results can be a pitfall which requires special attention. A typical analysis method is comparing the survey results with the results of another survey. It is highly recommended to check the differences in surveys before comparing them. Differences may arise from the method of data collection, type of questions or measurement scale. For typical examples of customer and staff surveys, see the Queensland Rail and Sony Australia case studies in Part II of this book.

Example (a)

Excellent	Good	Fair	Poor	Very poor
5	4	3	2	1

Example (b)

Strongly agree	Agree	Neither agree nor disagree	Disagree	Strongly disagree
5	4	3	2	1

Example (c)

Significantly above	Above	Met	Below	Significantly below
5	4	3	2	1

Example (d)

Very satisfied	Satisfied	Neither satisfied nor dissatisfied	Dissatisfied	Very dissatisfied
5	4	3	2	1

Figure 2.4   Typical examples of a five-point scale

CUSTOMER VISITS

There are two types of customer visit: an employee from an organization visiting the customer(s) or the organization being visited by a customer.

A few years ago, I worked with a self-adhesive label printing company called Impresstik which used customer visits as one of its core strategies, to stay ahead of the competition. Following the simple motto 'First impression counts', the managing director and owner of the company ensured that everything possible was done to create an impression that his business was different in many ways: modern machinery, high-tech equipment, clean production environment and storage areas, well-trained employees and a major focus on safety. The company was receiving visits almost every week from existing and new customers, and the managing director was personally hosting every customer. The majority of customers were incredibly impressed.

When the company was certified to ISO 9000 quality standards, the entire staff was invited to celebrate the achievement at the Rosemount Winery in Hunter Valley, Australia, one of its first five customers. Before the celebrations began, the staff were given a tour of the wine bottling plant where they could observe how the labels were applied to wine bottles and what problems the customer had with the labels. It was a brilliant idea to combine the celebration of an achievement with the study of problems on customer's production lines. In the following three consecutive years, Impresstik won the Supplier of the Year Award from Orlando Wynyard, its second largest customer.

Businesses like this printing company use customer visits to create a customer experience for their employees and provide an experience for their customers too. As seen from the Impresstik experience, when customer visits are used as a marketing strategy they can also lead to increased bottom-line results and continued growth.

FOCUS GROUPS

Focus groups are small groups, typically comprising of five to eight current or potential customers, who are asked in a similar fashion to customer interviews or customer surveys, to comment on the company or its products and services. Responses collected from focus groups, however, may differ from interviews and questionnaires as they are generated in a group environment. Many organizations, for instance, invite a number of selected customers to breakfast or lunch sessions conducted with company directors in order to listen to first-hand information and understand the nature of any problems. These sessions can also be used for building relationships with customers.

An Australian state-wide transport organization used focus groups to explore how well they were meeting customer needs. During these meetings, which were attended by the customer and the organization's front-line staff, it was discovered that one customer's major complaint was that an orange juice product was out of date before it reached the supermarket shelves. From this first-hand information a project was initiated where a team of the transport organization's staff, in partnership with the customer, re-engineered the delivery process to create a separate, specially expedited delivery process for all perishable products including the orange juice.

Focus groups assist the detailed exploration of situations at both supplier and customer ends, a better understanding of each other's business and the speeding up of process improvements.

MYSTERY SHOPPERS

Many service businesses, such as the banks and retail chains, often make use of mystery shoppers in order to obtain objective information about their services at the front line. 'Mystery shoppers' are professionals employed by the same organization, by market research companies or by hired contractors. As with other methods, the mystery shopper evaluation system has its limitations and should not be used without careful consideration of the benefits and shortfalls. Common problems associated with the mystery shopper system include the relative higher cost and small sample size. Where possible, many companies use also a mystery caller system as it is less expensive and assists in obtaining a larger sample size. Both systems require careful planning and special attention when being performed.

MARKET TREND ANALYSIS

Market trend analyses are typically performed by firms or government agencies specializing in market research on a regular basis. The results are usually published and can be viewed free of charge (online or in libraries) or are available for a small fee. Market trend information sources may also include customer and consumer associations, consumer journals, government and university websites, national and international trade organizations. Typical areas of market trend analysis include:

- market demand
- historic market performance
- market forecast
- price history and trends
- market analysis by sectors
- consumer analysis.

WARRANTY FORMS

Like an insurance policy, a 'warranty' is a form of assurance given in writing to customers that a particular product (or service) will perform as specified or is 'fit for the purposes for which it is intended'. Reasons for returning goods or warranty claims are an excellent source of information for finding out product performance shortcomings or why customers dislike certain features.

CUSTOMER COMPLAINTS

Listening to customer complaints is another way of exploring customer needs. In a staff satisfaction questionnaire, call centre operators were asked to comment on what the least pleasing part of their job is. Here is an example of the answers given: 'I enjoy working with customers but sometimes they can be quite annoying'. Unfortunately, this view is common in the service industry. Customers are the purpose of and not the annoying factor in the business. Every customer complaint should be viewed as an opportunity, not a problem. Staff attitudes toward customers and their needs can only improve if they learn to appreciate that a complaint is the result of an unsatisfactory situation and that a complaining customer provides an opportunity to the company to change dissatisfaction into satisfaction.

Typical things to consider when dealing with complaints include:

- develop a customer complaint handling procedure (which may include service recovery)
- select staff for customer service jobs who have the aptitude to work well with customers
- train staff in customer needs and how to face and handle complaints positively
- ensure that complaints are recorded so that they can be properly analysed and rectified by appropriate employees.

These days, many organizations use customer hotlines (phone or Internet) and encourage their customers to tell them what they like or dislike about their products or services. Using a centralized complaints database, companies are able not only to respond to complaints faster and reduce variation in complaint handling (service improvement) but also to reduce cost. Electronically recorded data also allow companies to analyse complaints better and track other useful information about product performance for end users.

BENCHMARKING

Identifying customer requirements through benchmarking usually involves other companies (benchmarks) and customer-related information which may be considered as sensitive or confidential. Per definition, 'benchmark' is a point of reference, something against which other things are measured or judged. In this context, benchmarking is the search for excellence, learning from the best in class. Typical steps of benchmarking include:

1. Defining areas for improvement
2. Identifying the benchmark
3. Measurement and collection of data
4. Adopting the data and
5. Follow up.

Measuring the *right* thing

When we are preparing to measure customer requirements (or the drivers of customer satisfaction), the first question we ask is whether we are measuring the right thing (metrics). The most important factor in identifying the metrics is customer perception. Does the metrics reflect what is important for the customers? Other factors that can be taken into consideration include resource availability, measurement complexity and cost. This is why market research companies usually explore things that are important to specific customers in interviews or focus groups before they design a survey questionnaire.

In *Moment of Truth* Jan Carlzon comments:

> The SAS cargo division had always measured its performance by the amount of freight carried, or how well they filled up the [passenger] planes' bellies. We soon realized that we had been measuring the wrong thing – an 'executive suite' goal that had nothing to do with the needs of our cargo customers. Indeed, our cargo customers were more concerned about *precision* or prompt deliveries to the specified locations.[2]

After identifying the right metrics, the company developed a suitable measurement and monitoring system called QualiCargo and improved its delivery accuracy up to 92 per cent.

Once the right metrics are defined, employees who are directly involved in the measurement process should be made aware of the following:

- the importance of the metrics to your organization
- the reasons behind the selection of the metrics
- how the metrics will be measured.

Every measurement system should also have a closed feedback loop. It is not only important that the right metrics is measured but also that customers and employees should be provided with feedback. The next step in the process of capturing the voice of the customer is to rank all requirements in order to identify which ones are more critical. This strategic analysis may also take into consideration the view of the organization, the 'voice of the business' (VOB). A typical VOB may include:

- resource availability
- competitive pressure
- market trends
- technical complexity
- technology availability
- cost of implementation.

Understanding the process thinking

In general, all organizations can be considered as systems comprising many components interacting with each other and creating synergies. The main components of such a system include people, products (and/or services) and processes. Organizations also have a culture and values and use certain strategies and tactics to achieve their vision and mission. In this context, 'business processes' can be defined as connected activities and actions organizations implement in order to achieve their goals and objectives. Process thinking is increasingly becoming popular among quality practitioners and other disciplines including information technology, engineering and management.

Process thinking is also the underlying concept behind Six Sigma; being a methodology that enables organizations to increase their overall efficiency and effectiveness in meeting goals and objectives. Within Six Sigma, process thinking starts with top management, who identify key processes and define ownership for them, conduct gap analysis based on process performance and on customer needs and allocate resources to improve those processes that impact on customer satisfaction and thus on bottom-line results.

In the following sections, the fundamental difference between products and services, and between manufacturing and non-manufacturing processes, will be discussed in further detail. We will also discuss some of the principles underlying the process thinking concept and provide answers to many questions, including:

- How do we define processes?
- How do we map processes?

- How do we measure and improve processes?

Manufacturing *versus* non-manufacturing

A useful working definition of 'manufacturing' can be found in the Australia and New Zealand Standard Industrial Classification (ANZSIC).[3] According to ANZSIC, manufacturing can be defined as 'the physical or chemical transformation of materials or components into new products'. This can be an automated, a semi-automated or a manual transformation. Therefore, manufacturing often involves a combination of machinery, tools, equipment, power and labour in order to bring materials to the desired product state. Typical manufacturing activities include design and development of products, production and/or assembly, inspection and testing of products. Due to the fact that manufacturing activities deal predominantly with products, manufacturing industries are usually grouped into the following product categories:

- primary and fabricated metal products
- chemical products
- industrial and commercial machinery
- electronic and electrical equipment
- automotive and transportation equipment
- wood and textile products
- printed and published media.

In the last few decades, we have witnessed an increasing degree of transformation in the industrialized economies; namely, a shift from typical manufacturing to non-manufacturing/service activities. In most of these countries, the majority of the workforce is now employed by the non-manufacturing industries which often account for more than two thirds of the gross domestic product (GDP).

According to the ANZSIC, any category other than manufacturing can be classified as 'non-manufacturing'. However, it is important to note that construction and mining industries are treated as separate categories within ANZSIC. Typical examples of non-manufacturing categories include:

- transportation and communication
- electricity, gas and sanitary services
- wholesale and retail trade
- finance, insurance and real estate
- service industries.

Service industries are further divided into sub-categories including:

- hospitality and recreation
- health and care for the elderly
- legal and accounting
- education and public administration.

Both manufacturing and non-manufacturing organizations employ processes that are common to both sectors. These processes are usually of transactional or service nature. Typical transactional or service processes may include:

- sales and marketing
- inquiry handling and order processing
- forecasting and production planning
- accounting and procurement
- budgeting and management (financial) reporting
- inventory and warehousing
- distribution and transportation
- pre-sales or after-sales service
- customer relationship management
- human resource management.

Most manufacturing processes are concerned with *tangible* outcomes as they deal with a physical product (look, touch and feel). In contrast, transactional and service processes are *less tangible*, as the physical product is often non-existent or difficult to discern. Some typical reasons why transactional or service processes can be problematic are:

- processes are usually not well defined
- processes are often poorly documented
- the measurement of process output is inconsistent or ill-defined
- processes often cross boundaries between departments or functional areas
- processes are usually perceived as 'cost centres' rather than 'profit centres'.

Product *versus* service

Products and services can be in any form: hardware, software or both. In general, products or goods are 'items' while service can be defined as 'work' that is performed for someone else. Categories of service may include:

- pre-sales service (product information, product training, and so on)
- after-sales service (product information, spare parts and repair, and so on)
- personal service (cleaning, laundry, leisure and recreation, travel, and so on)
- professional service (medical, education, consulting, contracting, and so on)
- government service (community, welfare, healthcare, defence, and so on).

Service can be performed online, off line or both. Since the introduction of the Internet, online service has been steadily increasing. Examples of typical online services (often referred to as 'e-service') include:

- banking and insurance
- education and training
- customer service
- accounting and finance

- entertainment (including games)
- communication (including publications)
- shopping.

Every product or service, whether consumed immediately or used over a period of time, is an outcome of a process. One of the main characteristics of service is that the service provider is often in contact with the customer. In most cases, these contacts are individual transactions. And every transaction has an impact on the customer. Service can be tangible, intangible or a combination of both. In general, service has three main tangible features or aspects:

- quality features
- delivery aspect
- price.

Quality features are usually more difficult to measure than delivery and price. As a matter of fact, depending on the type of service, some quality features are more difficult to measure than others; and for the customer, some quality features are more important than others.
    Tangible service features include:

- conformance (specification)
- service delivery (access time, action time, queuing time, and so on)
- value for money (more volume, more weight, free extras, and so on)
- courtesy (attitude)
- user friendliness (simplicity)
- well-being (atmosphere, safety, hygiene, and so on).

Intangible service features include:

- personal preference (smell, taste, colour choice, and so on)
- feelings of importance, privilege, social responsibility, and so on.

Defining the process

Whatever the characteristics are, manufacturing as well as transactional or service processes all have one thing in common; they are *processes*. A typical process has a start, an end and a purpose, and is usually linked to other processes. Every process has inputs and outputs. A process can be defined as 'a set of interrelated activities and tasks that transform inputs into outputs by adding value'.
    As illustrated in Figure 2.5, the input-process-output (IPO) model will be used throughout the book to describe process. Every process can be measured, analysed and improved. Some of the tools and techniques used within Six Sigma to improve manufacturing processes may differ from those for improving transactional or service processes; however, the fundamentals are the same.
    Figure 2.5 illustrates the application of an IPO model to a typical non-manufacturing process. In this example, selling products is the process; products sold and information provided to customers are the outputs; and staff training, forecast accuracy and inventory

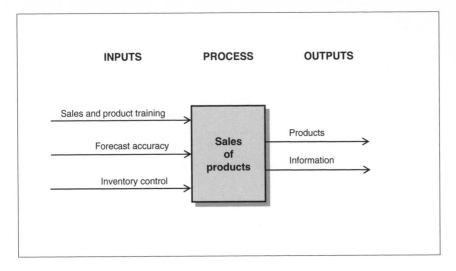

Figure 2.5   Input-process-output model applied to a transactional process

control are the inputs. To evaluate the process performance, and determine whether the process requires improvement, we need to identify the process metrics. Typical metrics for a sales process include: product quality, product availability, delivery time and delivery accuracy.

The IPO model is a very simple but powerful graphic tool for identifying the process and its inputs and outputs. It can be very useful for implementing a 'process-based approach' in the organization. Today, most companies use organizational charts which comprise functional management structures rather than process-based structures. Organizational charts and position descriptions are mainly used to describe a business function rather than the processes which make up that function. They might be useful for defining the 'chain of command'; however, they don't show how organizations work or what processes are in place to produce a product or deliver a service.

In one of the organizations I worked with, customer returns were understood to be one of the key processes. However, top management was not aware who exactly was responsible for this process. In this example, the sales division was dealing with the customers. However, customer returns were processed by the finance division. After extensive discussions it was determined that this process should be owned by the sales division as the staff in sales division were in direct contact with the end customer, while the finance had an indirect relationship.

In most cases, it is easy to identify the owner of a particular process. In other cases, it might be more difficult to identify the appropriate process owner. As a rule of thumb, *process knowledge is often used as the key criterion in determining the process owners.*

Mapping the process

A 'process map' or 'process diagram' is basically a set of graphic symbols (boxes and arrows) that provide essential information about the nature of a process. Information obtained from a process map usually includes:

- process boundaries and links
- process owners
- process inputs and outputs
- process customers and suppliers.

One of the common mistakes with process mapping is that people try to map everything and therefore lose track of the 'big picture'. It can become quite messy if it is done without a plan. Depending on the objectives, it should be clearly stated what level of detail is needed before mapping the processes. Deciding which processes to map depends on several factors. The following questions will assist in developing a list of selection criteria:

- Is the process a core competency?
- Is the process outcome (quality and delivery performance) satisfactory for customers?
- Is the process still required after considering the technology changes?
- Is the process still required after considering mergers and acquisitions?
- Are there any competitive reasons to maintain the process?

Process maps are useful tools for:

- understanding the processes as the basis for process analysis and improvement
- pinpointing problem areas and opportunities for improvements
- communicating work or process requirements
- training staff, particularly new employees, in how to perform the work.

In general, we can differentiate between two types of process mapping: macro process mapping and micro process mapping. The two most commonly used methods for process mapping are the process flow (PF) chart and the cross-functional (CF) process map. In basic, the IPO model is a simplified process map which can be used in conjunction with the PF chart and CF process map.

A process flow (PF) chart is a graphical representation of material or information flow within a process. It illustrates the steps and activities of a workflow from start to finish in sequential order. It shows the inputs and outputs, pathways, action and decision points. Common symbols used in flowcharting include:

- box (an activity or action)
- diamond (decision)
- oval (start or end)
- arrow (pathway).

Figure 2.6 depicts the use of a linear process flow chart for a simplified manufacturing process, from receiving the customer order through to despatch of products. As this is a high-level flow chart, each step may require separate flowcharting. Process flow charts illustrate the flow within the process, but do not necessarily show how the process steps are measured or controlled and what the specific inputs and outputs are. This can be achieved by combining the IPO model and the linear flow chart as depicted in Figure 2.7.

Cross-functional process maps are often a preferred flowcharting method if more than

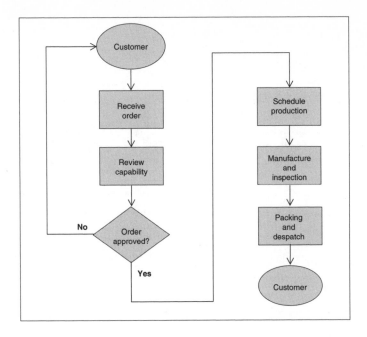

Figure 2.6   Example of a process flow chart

one entity or department is involved in the process. In Figure 2.8 a cross-functional process map has been used to illustrate the process of staff training.

Measuring and analysing the process

Processes are measured by three types of metrics: quality, time and monetary metrics. In the transactional and service processes, one of the most commonly used metrics is time metrics. At a bank counter or for a delivery service, for instance, waiting time is one of the most annoying aspects of the service for the customer. Customers feel the difference if the service is performed quickly or slowly, and they value prompt and speedy service. Typical time metrics may include:

- elapsed time
- cycle time
- lead time
- idle time
- transportation time
- delivery time
- waiting time
- product freshness (storage time)
- delays.

Other metrics that are often used in the transactional and service environments include:

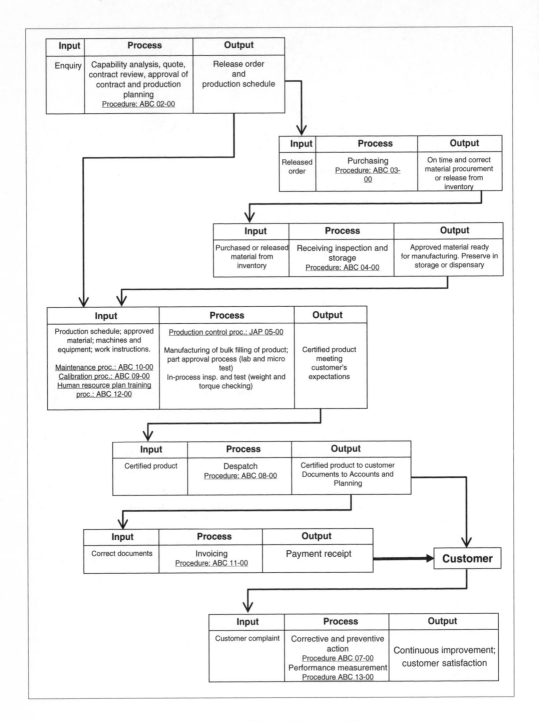

Figure 2.7   Example of a combination of the IPO model and the PF chart

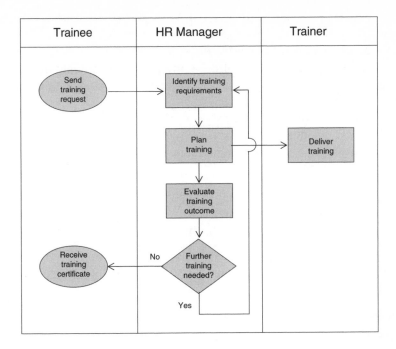

Figure 2.8   Example of a cross-functional map

- monetary metrics (for example sales volume, profit margin, cost of returns, inventory levels, and so on)
- information, product or service quality metrics (for example number of complaints, number of errors made in transactions, number of returns, and so on).

When analysing transactional and service processes, the following questions assist the identification of areas for improvement:

- Which steps are critical to the process outcome?
- How long does it take to complete the entire process and the critical steps?
- Which are the weakest links?
- Are there any repeated or duplicated steps?
- Are there any unnecessary steps in the process?
- Which steps add (extra) cost to the process?

The Six Sigma toolbox has substantial analytical tools that can be used for determining the metrics and measuring and analysing processes. This is discussed in further detail in Chapters 3 and 5.

Summary

The foundations of Six Sigma consist of the two prime elements:

- customer and
- process.

There are two types of customers: internal customers and external customers. The external customer may be a final customer or an intermediate customer. It is fundamentally important that the customer be first identified and the voice of the customer (VOC) be captured. Capturing the VOC requires a sound understanding of the customer's requirements. A tool for assisting this process is the Kano analysis. The VOC chart is a simple tool used to summarize the Kano principle.

Identifying the customer needs is established through:

- customer interviews
- customer survey questionnaires
- customer visits
- focus groups
- mystery shoppers/callers
- market trend analysis
- warranty claims
- customer complaints
- benchmarking.

Each of these procedures has its strengths and weaknesses and much care must be taken when undertaking them.

When measuring the customer's requirements, it is most important to identify if the *right* thing is being measured. The metrics coupled with the VOC and the voice of the business (VOB) is then used to identify the most critical customer requirements. Once 'the customer' and their critical requirements are identified, it then becomes necessary to identify the associated organizational processes that service the customer.

Within Six Sigma, processes are

- defined and owned
- mapped
- measured and improved.

Processes are defined as having

- inputs and outputs
- a start and an end
- a purpose and
- usually a link to other processes.

Most organizations use organizational charts that describe 'the chain of command' rather than the desired processes. An IPO model is the best method of describing one or more processes. A simple process map can be depicted using the IPO model. A flow chart depicts the 'flow' of activities involved in a process. To ensure the inclusion of process inputs, outputs and what process steps are being measured and controlled, the IPO model can be combined with the process flow chart. Cross-functional process maps are a special use of the linear process flow chart.

Processes are measured by the following metrics:

- quality metrics
- time metrics and
- monetary metrics.

The Six Sigma toolbox includes substantial analytical tools for determining metrics and measuring/analysing the processes.

Notes

1. Jan Carlzon (1989) *Moments of Truth*. New York: Harper and Row, page 24.
2. *Ibid.*, page 107.
3. The ANZSIC can be found at: http://www.abs.gov.au/ausstats

3 *Six Sigma Projects*

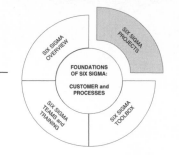

Introduction

In Chapter 2, we discussed customers and process thinking as being the foundations of Six Sigma. Other aspects of the Six Sigma methodology include project management, measurement and improvement, and management and staff involvement.

In this chapter we will discuss in detail what Six Sigma projects are and how they are used to measure, analyse and improve processes. The strength of Six Sigma comes from its underlying concept process thinking. It recognizes that organizations consist of processes and outputs of these processes are delivered to internal and external customers, and that processes must be constantly reviewed and improved where necessary to ensure customer satisfaction. Six Sigma projects are the vehicle used by Six Sigma teams to implement this thinking. Six Sigma projects, often referred to as the Black Belt or Green Belt projects (the Six Sigma Belt levels are discussed in Chapter 4) are not stand-alone projects but are directly linked to organizational goals and objectives, as shown in Chapter 1.

A typical Six Sigma project has five phases: Define, Measure, Analyse, Improve and Control. This is commonly referred to as the DMAIC methodology, as depicted in Figure 3.1.

In the define phase, the improvement area (process) is identified and project requirements such as project time frame, team membership and necessary resources are

Project phase	Activities
Define CTQ	• Identify the need for improvement • Define project requirements
Measure Metrics (Y)	• Measure performance of process • Pinpoint the problem sources and areas for improvement
Analyse Vital Fews (X)	• Identify root causes of problems or critical factors for improvement
Improve Optimal condition	• Identify and implement problem solutions or actions for improvement
Control Standardization	• Ensure that new process conditions (process changes) are stable • Standardize the new process and share key learnings

Figure 3.1 Six Sigma project phases and their corresponding activities

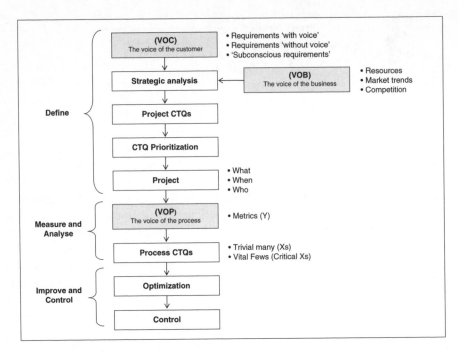

Figure 3.2   A typical Six Sigma project flow diagram

defined. In the measure and analyse phases, data are collected and analysed to determine changes to the process in order to achieve a desired outcome. These changes are then implemented in the improve phase, while in the control phase actions are taken to ensure that process changes are stable and the process does not return to its original condition. The flow of these activities and their relationship with each other is shown Figure 3.2. Note how the voice of the customer (VOC) and voice of the business (VOB) play an active and important role in the strategic analysis.

Within Six Sigma, the DMAIC is the most commonly used methodology for process improvement. In some cases, however, another version of DMAIC called DFSS (Design For Six Sigma) is used when designing and/or introducing a new product or service. Simply put, DFSS applies the Six Sigma concepts specifically to design processes by using a methodology called DMADV (Define, Measure, Analyse, Design and Verify). In principle, DMAIC and DMADV use the same methodology but apply different tools and methods. In this book, the focus has been put on the DMAIC methodology which is discussed in greater detail in the following sections.

Project Phase Define

Identify the need for improvement
Define project requirements

Define is perhaps the most critical phase within any Six Sigma project. Many aspects need to be thoroughly analysed before an improvement effort can be committed. These aspects include the VOC, the current state of the process, resource availability and benefits for the business.

The identification of a need for improvement, namely the selection of the *right* Six Sigma project, is one of the critical activities in the define phase. There is always a potential risk associated with project selection. Projects may not be completed within a scheduled time frame or may take up more resources than planned. It is also likely that a project does not have the predicted impact on business results or achieves only a small or insignificant improvement to a process. If a project is not realistic, it will lead to frustration for everyone involved and ensure a decline in motivation for Black Belts and Green Belts. Projects selected on the basis of experience, gut feeling or courage have a higher risk than a project carefully chosen on the basis of data analysis. Selecting a wrong project may result in financial losses to the organization and increasing personnel dissatisfaction. On the other hand, if the right project is selected, everyone will benefit: shareholders, personnel and customers.

As mentioned earlier, project selection starts with an identification of a need for improvement. Whether you are in manufacturing or non-manufacturing operations, as a starting point you can look at a company's performance results in areas such as:

- market share
- sales volume
- customer complaints
- staff turnover
- employee complaints.

When searching for potential projects in the transactional and service environments, the areas to investigate may include:

- customer service
- returned goods and warranty process
- accounts receivable and accounts payable
- distribution and supply chain
- inventory and warehousing
- computer networks.

As part of the project selection process, preliminary data must be collected and analysed to identify an improvement area. Data don't always have to be numeric but they should be specific and quantifiable. Most organizations collect data in some form about their customers, staff and suppliers. This information might be not readily available as it is often collected by different divisions and stored at different locations. However, the data are usually there and available. The point to be made is that these data need to be analysed in order to identify which area or process requires an urgent improvement. In Six Sigma terminology, the improvement area (or the process to be improved) is commonly referred to as the Critical to Quality (CTQ).

A very useful mechanism for identifying CTQs is a cause-and-effect (CE) diagram. Like many other tools within Six Sigma, CE diagrams can be used for multiple purposes. As a problem-solving tool, the CE diagram is commonly used for identifying the factors which are believed to be contributing to the project outcome, and are therefore key sources of worthwhile actions to achieve a positive effect. In other words, the CE diagram can identify the factors which might be causing a problem. Some factors have a greater impact on the project outcome than others.

Once a process at higher level has been singled out as the area for improvement, the next question to be asked is: what portions of the process actually require further improvement? While the following project phases – measure and analyse – will provide detailed answers to this question, it is advisable to conduct a preliminary analysis at the define phase in order to identify the improvement metrics.

A preliminary analysis may be carried out by using the data available. This information typically includes customer complaints, trends charts, process maps, and procedures and work instruction. Most organizations, these days, maintain a certified quality management system which requires organizations to identify and document their key processes. Many organizations adopt the process flow chart as a visual form of process documentation. Other data sources may include input-process-output diagrams, customer specifications, product catalogues, organizational/functional charts and position descriptions.

When it comes to selection of Six Sigma projects, one of the key concerns is how to prioritize potential projects (CTQs). One prioritization mechanism is the QFD (quality-function deployment) chart. As mentioned earlier, within Six Sigma many quality improvement tools are for multiple purposes. QFD, for instance, is also known as 'The House-of-Quality' and is commonly used by many organizations to translate customer requirements into product or service design requirements. But it can also be used as a prioritization vehicle. How to prioritize projects with a simplified QFD chart is demonstrated in Figure 3.3. (Note: the 'roof' (correlation matrix) and the boxes 'competitive' and 'technical analysis of a typical QFD' have been removed in order to simplify it and focus on the central part of the chart.)

As a first step, CTQs are entered in the top part of the chart. When defining selection

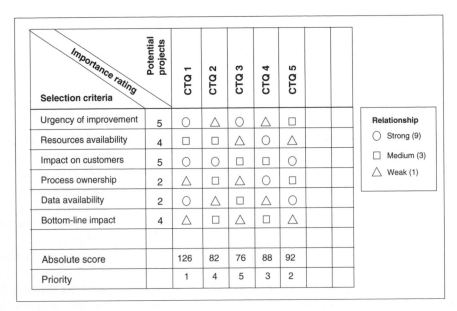

Figure 3.3   Example of CTQ prioritization by using a simplified QFD chart

criteria and importance rating, it is crucial that consideration be given to the type and nature of the business. Some criteria are generic and can be used by all types of organizations or divisions within the organization; others are more specific and applicable to certain divisions or functions. It is therefore important that each division define its own selection criteria representing the actual business processes within the division.

The relationship between CTQs and selection criteria is then expressed by a numeric symbol ranging from weak to strong. Chosen relationship numbers are then multiplied with 'importance ratings' and the result in each column summed as an 'absolute score'. Highest absolute scoring projects should be given highest priority.

CTQs can be directly transformed into projects if required. However, in most cases, CTQs (or potential projects) identified at a business level are difficult to manage (they are too vague or too large) and therefore must be broken down to the operational and process level. This is made possible by the use of the CE chart, as mentioned in Chapter 1. In such a case, the business plan can be converted into a simple CE chart which would highlight only those factors which are considered to be important for achieving business objectives (see also the Sony case study in Part II).

After a strategic analysis and the identification of the CTQs, major emphasis must be placed on the project teams. When forming the teams, the most important aspect by far is team leadership. In most cases, team leadership is assigned to a 'Black Belt'. That's why most Six Sigma projects are often referred to as the 'Black Belt projects'. As well as Black Belt projects, some organizations also use 'Green Belt projects'. These projects (typically assigned to Green Belts) have less complexity and are completed in a shorter time than Black Belt projects. Then there is also another Six Sigma project type called 'the Quick Shot project', which is only used by a small number of organizations to capture ideas or suggestions for processes improvement. As with the project selection process, assigning one or more Black Belts to a project requires the consideration of a number of criteria, including resource availability, technical and leadership skills, just to name a few. Further information on Six Sigma teams, various Six Sigma roles and their responsibilities can be found in Chapter 4.

One of the most critical aspects of a Six Sigma project is that it must always have a champion who owns the project. One of main tasks of the champion is to clarify the scope of the project with the project leader in order to avoid misinterpretations and false starts. The project scope should be as concise as possible and include numerical measurement values for the deliverables. Most Six Sigma companies use a project description form which not only identifies the project characteristics but also provides a register of the project for better tracking (Figure 3.4).

The project charter is another important requirement of a Six Sigma project as it identifies the roles and activities of a project team. In a typical Black Belt project, members will consist of Green Belts and personnel within a department. Cross-functional projects may also include personnel from different divisions. Working in teams isn't always easy. Some project teams usually get on well, others face enormous difficulties within the team. Tasks, communication rules, meetings and other requirements should be clearly defined in a project charter to avoid unnecessary confusion.

Most Six Sigma projects result in changes to the processes which may cause some resistance from a number of sources at some phase. It is important that the potential resistance is clearly identified before a project starts. One common method of identifying resistance is the stakeholder analysis. Stakeholders of a process may include internal or external customers, the process owner and other employees. It is critical that process

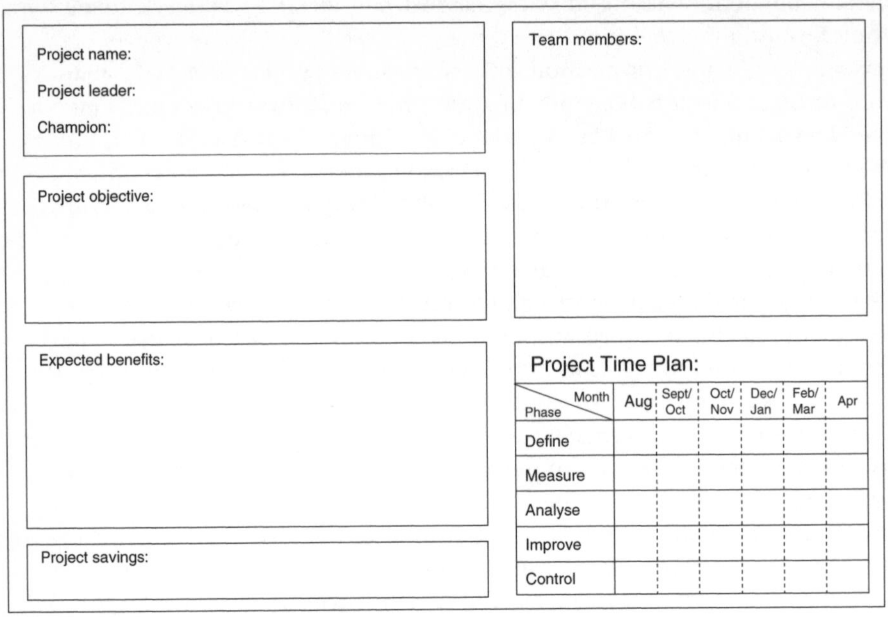

Figure 3.4   Example of a typical Six Sigma project registration form

changes, including their benefits, are clearly communicated to all stakeholders in a timely fashion in order to avoid confusion and criticism.

Project Phase Measure

Measure performance of the process
Pinpoint the problem sources and areas for improvement

The measure phase consists of the following main activities:

- data collection
- the charting of data
- measurement system analysis (MSA).

One of the main objectives of the measure phase is to understand the current state of the process. In basic, Six Sigma is always about measuring and improving the performance of processes. We won't know how processes perform until they are measured. Measurement usually involves the collection and charting of data. Data doesn't always have to be actual numeric values, but it should be in the form of specific and quantifiable information.

DATA COLLECTION

Most organizations collect and maintain sufficient data in some form about their customers, staff and suppliers. This information might not always be readily available as it is often collected by different divisions and stored at different locations. However, the information is usually there.

There are two types of measures: 'hard' measures, mostly used in manufacturing processes, and 'soft' measures, mainly used in transactional and service environments. Hard measures are tangible, are based on concrete facts and are objective data (for example product dimensions). Soft measures are often intangible, based on perceptions and therefore subjective (for example customer and employee satisfaction). However, there are common techniques to quantify subjective information. One typical example of such a technique is the customer and employee survey questionnaires where responses (subjective information) are transformed into numeric values through the allocation of scores.

Before collecting any process information, it is advisable to have a plan for data collection and to include in it important issues such as:

- What kind of data is needed?
- What is the intended purpose of the data collection?
- Are the data relevant and representative for the process?
- How much data is sufficient?
- What is the method and time span of data collection?

Data collection requires specific or certain knowledge about basic analysis methods including statistics. One of the important things to know about data collection is that there are two types of data to be collected: continuous data and discrete data. Continuous data are obtained from a system or process, through measurement or calculation. Discrete data are obtained by observations and counts of occurrences or non-occurrences.

Typical continuous data in a manufacturing environment, for instance, may include the measurement of the product and process parameters, such as product dimensions, process temperature, process speed and weight of ingredients. Discrete data in a manufacturing environment may include the number of defective products, type of defects, number of machine malfunctions and the number of customer complaints. Continuous data in transactional and service environments may include cycle time or lead time of a particular process or transaction, sales figures and length of customer calls. Typical discrete data in transactional and service environments may include type and number of applications, number of incorrect transactions and number of complaints.

There are many tools and other mechanisms that can be used to collect meaningful information about service and transactional processes. One of the commonly used tools for the manual collection of discrete data is the check list. A typical check list consists of a list of characteristics to be observed and a field to record the number of occurrences for each characteristic (Figure 3.5).

CHARTING DATA

Charting or plotting the collected data is the next step of process characterization. Some of the most commonly used charts in the transactional and service environments are:

- Pareto charts
- frequency plots (histograms) and
- run charts

Error code	Number of occurrences	Rank
Wrong amount charged	32	A
Late completion and postage	13	B
Sent to wrong company	5	C
Sent to wrong person	3	D
Lost in mail	2	E

Figure 3.5   Example of a simple check list used for the collection of data on invoicing errors

Pareto charts

Pareto charts are simple to construct and provide a sound foundation for decision-making which makes them the preferred tool for data analysis in the transactional and service environments. Pareto charts can be used to:

- focus on a specific subject or problem
- analyse the problem and decide on improvement items (targets)
- take action, then determine the effect of the improvement by comparing the states before and after the action.

In a typical Pareto chart, data are usually plotted in categories in descending rank order of their frequencies. While the one axis portrays the absolute value for each category, the other axis shows the cumulative percentage of the frequencies (Figure 3.6).

One of the conclusions that can be drawn from the Pareto chart is the 80/20 rule. In general, 80 per cent of results are produced by 20 per cent of inputs. Typical examples of the 80/20 rule are:

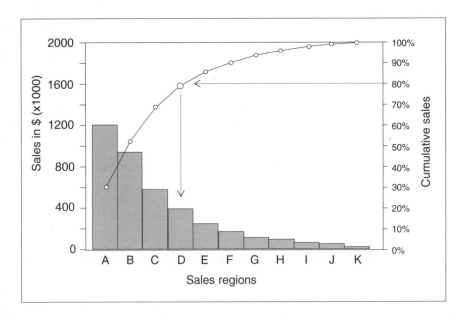

Figure 3.6   Example of a Pareto chart used for the identification of best performing sales regions

- 80 per cent of sales are obtained from 20 per cent of customers
- 80 per cent of all problems are due to 20 per cent of all causes

A practical interpretation of this principle is that a Pareto chart separates the 'vital few' (critical) items from the 'trivial many' and enables us to focus on those critical items. In Figure 3.6, for instance, the first four regions contribute to 80 per cent of the company's total sales. For further information on how to construct a Pareto chart see Chapter 5.

Frequency plots (histograms)

Frequency plots are often used to study the frequency (occurrence) characteristics of a particular data set. For this purpose, the observations will be arranged in such a way that they can be conveniently plotted over numerically ordered classes or categories. Frequency plots show the distribution of a data set, thus enabling us to study and compare the characteristics of various distributions. One of the most commonly used frequency plots is the histogram where individual data values are plotted as a bar (Figure 3.7). Further information on how to construct a histogram can be found in Chapter 5.

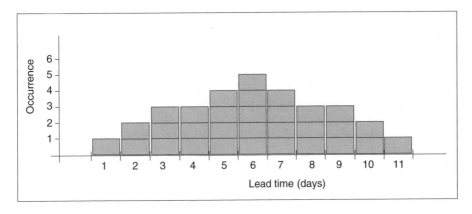

Figure 3.7   Example of a histogram used to display the distribution of lead times

Histograms are often used to study the characteristics of a process, the dispersion and central tendency, and compare them with specified requirements. They can be a useful tool for comparative analysis of data obtained from different processes or before and after a change made to a process.

Run charts

Run charts are also called 'time plots' or 'trend charts' as they display the occurrence of an event over a specified period of time. In a way, run charts are very similar to control charts (explained in Project Phase Control). However, run charts don't display the acceptable limits (control limits) of a process. The aim in using a run chart is to see the trend in data and whether any unusual patterns, such as peaks and lows, occur in the process. A typical example of a run chart obtained from sales data is shown in Figure 3.8.

MEASUREMENT SYSTEM ANALYSIS

The aim of a measurement system analysis is the validation of the collected information.

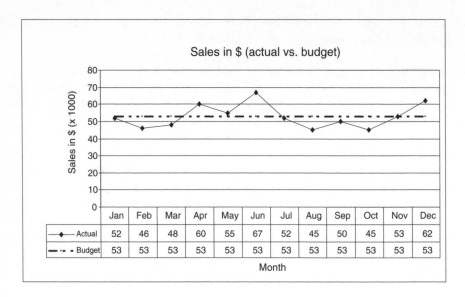

Figure 3.8   Example of a run chart of a sales process

There are a number of common problems that may occur when collecting data from a process or system. For instance, data may be inaccurate, imprecise or not producible. The aim of the measurement system analysis is the validation of the collected information. We usually assume that collected data represent a variation within the process and do not include any variations due to error in the way data are collected. This assumption, however, has to be validated before a conclusion can be drawn that the variation due to measurement error is negligible.

A typical measurement system consists of three components, a measurement device, the method of measurement and the personnel carrying out the measurement. The suitability of the measurement instrument, its precision and calibration are some of the typical errors associated with a measurement device. Measurement method related errors may include wrong sampling procedure and inaccurate instructions. Insufficient training or lack of attention are some of the common errors that occur due to human factors.

For many people, it seems that this concept is difficult to adopt outside of the manufacturing environments due to lack of use of a typical measurement device to collect data. Precision or calibration of a device often has no meaning in non-manufacturing areas.

However, in transactional and service processes, we may use other means to collect data from processes. Whether it is the processing time for a particular transaction or the quality of the service output, most companies collect numerical data about their transactional and service processes and record them somewhere. The question is: 'How are the data collected, measured and recorded?' Nowadays, most transactional processes are carried out with the aid of computerized systems (hardware and software) which allow us to measure the processing time quite accurately. However, how do we know whether the information being entered in, say, a spreadsheet is accurate? In an accounts payable department, for instance, there are several personnel who enter data into computerized systems and manipulate them where necessary.

One of the typical means of collecting service-related data is surveying the recipients of those processes. The end user would be the recipient of a service in many cases. However, there are also a vast number of processes in every company which do not deliver services to end users. The human resource division, for instance, is one of those business functions that delivers support services to internal customers: employees and their managers.

Whether the recipients of a service are internal customers (for example employees) or external customers (for example end users), customer satisfaction is one of the key process outputs in which we are interested. We usually measure customer satisfaction through surveys by using some sort of questionnaire. A questionnaire is an instrument (like a measurement device in manufacturing) that can be used to collect data from various sources.

Testing the validity of a questionnaire can be performed in many ways. 'Validity' means we are satisfied with the instrument and that it measures what it is supposed to measure. In the case of a survey, we can validate the questionnaire by testing it with someone or some group who are not part of the survey team before sending it out to the actual respondents.

Regardless of the type of measurement instrument (it can be a measurement device or a customer survey questionnaire), we are interested in capturing data that is accurate, not biased, repeatable, stable and reproducible. More information on accuracy, repeatability and reproducibility can be found in Chapter 5.

Project Phase Analyse

Identify the root cause(s) of the problem or critical factors for improvement

In the analyse phase, we will identify the root cause(s) or source(s) of problem or the critical factors which will enable us to achieve an improvement target.

As mentioned in earlier sections, Six Sigma is a robust quality and process improvement concept which requires sound process analysis. The following are recommended for the typical analysis of a process:

- the use of the input-process-output (IPO) model
- process mapping
- root cause analysis
- identifying problem solutions or actions for improvement.

As we discussed in Chapter 2, a 'process' can be defined as 'a set of activities that transform inputs into outputs with the aim of adding value'. In every process, some entities provide the inputs (supplier) and some entities receive the outputs (customers). A simple IPO model can assist in identifying the key ingredients of a process. Figure 3.9 illustrates an example of IPO model and how it is applied to a training process.

While the IPO model helps in identifying and focusing on the key elements or ingredients of a process, a flow chart shows the material or information flow within the process. Figure 3.10 depicts a process flow (PF) chart of a training process.

Once the process is mapped and the problem area is identified, the next step is to conduct a root cause analysis to find out the possible causes of the problem. One of the most commonly used tools for identifying the root causes of a problem is the cause-and-effect (CE) diagram. A typical CE diagram (also referred to as the Fishbone or Ishikawa diagram; see Chapter 1) has been used in Figure 3.11 to identify the root causes of a poor photocopy quality.

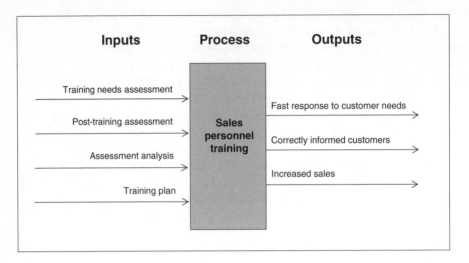

Figure 3.9   Example of an IPO model and its application to a training process

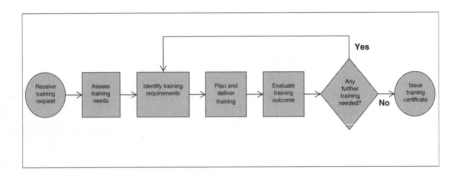

Figure 3.10   Example of a process flow chart applied to a training process

Root causes of a problem can be identified by using various techniques. One of the most commonly used techniques in obtaining root causes is brainstorming. Brainstorming sessions are usually conducted with a team of employees who have sufficient knowledge about the process. Brainstorming starts with idea generation. Team members are asked to generate as many ideas (root causes) as possible. It is important to ensure that there is no criticism of ideas during brainstorming sessions. Ideas should be judged and analysed once the brainstorming has finished

Figure 3.12 shows a selection of possible problem causes in a typical transactional and service environment where computerized office equipment is used to process business information.

Once the root causes have been identified and grouped, the team will then discuss and evaluate the relationship between the effect and each cause. Pareto diagrams, frequency plots and scatter diagrams are some of the frequently used tools for gathering additional information about the root causes. Other information sources may include run charts, test and survey results.

In some transactional and service environments, we might also want to improve a

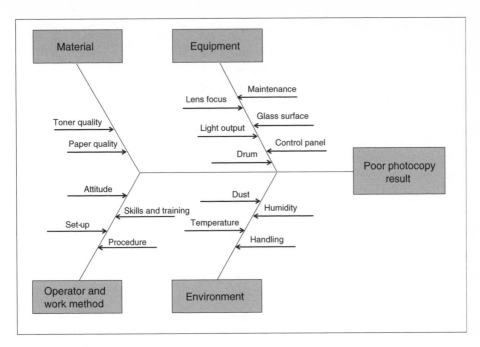

Figure 3.11   Example of the use of a cause-and-effect diagram

Information system	Method	Management	Staff	Environment
Set up	Procedures	Training	Training	Temperature
Power surge	Instruments	Skills	Skills	Stress
Data contamination	Set	Experience	Experience	Space
Compatibility		Attitude	Attitude	Lighting
Data storage		Communication	Communication	Humidity
Complexity				

Figure 3.12   Typical root cause of problems in an office environment

process that may not have an obvious problem. For instance, we might want to increase the sales performance for a particular item, reduce inventory or implement a new technology. Of course, the underlying assumption is there will always be something in every process that does not perform well and which can be fixed. For better illustration, we differentiate between problem-solving and the achievement of a target or goal.

Figure 3.13 shows how to use a CE chart to achieve a goal or an improvement target. In this example, increasing the efficiency of sales personnel training has been set as the improvement target. The project team has brainstormed all possible factors which impact on the target. These factors may have a negative or positive impact on the achievement target. It is expected that some factors will have a much higher impact than others. Those factors with higher impact are called 'critical factors'.

In Six Sigma terminology, process output is called the 'metric'. In mathematical

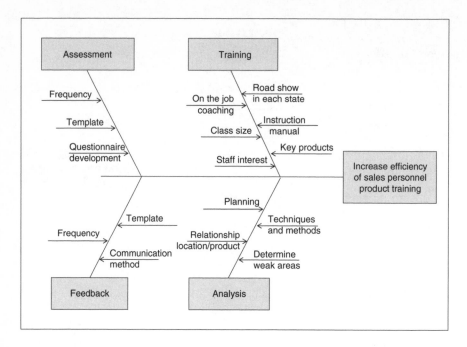

Figure 3.13   Example of the use of a CE chart to achieve a goal

terminology, the output can be expressed as 'Y', which is fully dependent on the variable 'X'. This is expressed as the formula: $Y = f(X)$. The 'Y' represents the output, 'X' the input, and 'f' (the function) is the process. There are usually many variables (Xs) which affect the output (Y). In Six Sigma terminology the Xs are called the 'Trivial Many'. Not all Xs have the same effect or impact on the output (Y); some are more significant than others. The objective of the analyse phase is to identify those factors with higher impact or the most likely root causes of the problem, the Vital Fews (Critical Xs).

There are a number of different ways of identifying the Vital Few factors. One simple method is to use a set of criteria for further analysis. Typical criteria may include:

- ease of control
- frequency of occurrence
- cost of implementation
- time frame of implementation
- urgency of implementation
- technology availability
- technical difficulty (complexity)
- organizational culture
- industrial relations.

In most cases, the project analyse phase will result in identification of a large number of critical factors (Vital Fews) which then need to be prioritized. As we discussed in the define phase, QFD is a simple and useful tool which can be used for the prioritization of Vital Fews.

Project Phase Improve

Identify and implement problem solutions or actions for improvement

In the improve phase, problem solutions (corrections to the process) are identified and implemented. There are various tools and forms which can be used to identify solutions to problem root causes. The failure-mode-effect-analysis (FMEA) chart is one of the valuable aids which can be used for this purpose. In its typical form, FMEA is usually used during the design of products or services to identify potential failures and their corrective actions. In this book, we use a simplified version of the FMEA chart to determine the improvement actions.

Figure 3.14 illustrates the use of a simplified FMEA to determine the improvement actions. In our example of a sales personnel training process, the following factors have been determined as critical (Vital Fews):

- staff interest
- assessment questionnaire and template.

Critical factors (Vital Fews)	Failure mode	Failure effects	Possible causes	Problem solution or action for improvement
Staff interest	Lack of interest in training	Poor training outcome	Lack of motivation	Information about training need, scope, effect and outcome to be made available to staff
	Lack of interest in training	Poor training outcome	Personal conflict	Provide individual consultation to staff and involve manager where needed
Assessment questionnaire and template	Format and content not suitable	Inaccurate results	Format and content requirements not determined in an appropriate manner	Format requirements and selection of questions to be determined and evaluated with the help of an expert

Figure 3.14   Example of a simplified FMEA chart used to identify actions for improvement

Before implementing corrective actions, it is advisable to use a planning tool to avoid unnecessary surprises. The Gantt chart is one of the most common vehicles for implementing actions. A typical Gantt chart lists, in a sequential order, the various tasks to be performed and their requirements including timing, duration, responsible person, and expected outcomes. Figure 3.15 illustrates the implementation of the improvement actions identified in Figure 3.14 by using a typical Gantt chart.

Project Phase Control

Ensure that new process conditions (process changes) are stable
Standardize the new process and share key learnings

Step	Task	Expected outcome	By when	By whom	Status
1	Develop questionnaire and assessment template	Appropriate templates	30 Jun	John	Completed
2	Develop training instruction manual	Training standardized	15 Jul	John	Draft completed
3	Analyse relationship btw product and location	Weaknesses identified	25 Jul	Mike	Completed
4	Develop roadshow	Presentation materials	10 Aug	Harry	In progress
5	Carry out initial survey	Training needs identified	24 Aug	Mike	In progress
6	Deliver first batch training	Satisfied trainees	15 Sept	John	In progress
7	Obtain feedback	Areas for further improvement identified	15 Sept	John	Planned

Figure 3.15   Example of the use of the Gantt chart to plan improvement actions

Once the necessary changes have been made to the process, the next step is to determine whether the process is stable after the implementation of those changes. In other words, we have to ensure that the same problem does not recur. For instance, we have carried out a project in order to reduce inventory for a particular product. But how can we ensure that the inventory remains at the improved level and does not increase again over the next few months? In other words, how do we sustain the benefits? And perhaps an equally important question is: how do we further improve the *new* process? What did we learn from this experience? How can we standardize the process and gain more from it? The objective of the control phase is to find answers to these questions.

One of the requirements for controlling a changed (improved) process is to capture new information in the process documentation. As mentioned earlier, PF charts and IPO diagrams must be updated immediately to reflect the changes in the process. Instructions manuals, procedures, work instructions and other process information materials should be included in the update.

In some transactional or service processes, it might be difficult to collect data due to various reasons. In these processes, indicators can be determined which would generate a corrective action if a result is negative. For instance, if a customer is not happy with the service provided at the counter, the counter staff may follow another set of instructions to satisfy the customer. In this example, customer's reaction is the indicator. The two extreme outcomes would be: happy or unhappy. In this example, it is not only necessary to clearly determine the indicator but it is also crucial to define the method of monitoring the indicator and how to respond to extreme situations, for instance, and to the negative reaction in particular. Such indicators and their monitoring methods and corresponding responses can be added to the PF charts. Additional information about process indicators and monitoring methods would make these documents an extremely valuable tool for staff training and process improvement.

Almost every process exhibits some degree of variability. Control charts can be used to investigate and understand the nature of variability. Sources of variability can be divided into two categories: the common causes and the special causes. Special causes are those causes that occur occasionally and can be assigned to special circumstances (for instance, an unexpected computer crash due to a power failure that occurred only once in a long period of time). Special causes usually affect the process output more than common causes and can be easily detected by a control chart. Typical examples of special causes in the transactional and service environments include:

- differences between personnel (one person is different from the rest for physical, cultural, educational, psychological or emotional reasons)
- differences between data processing equipment(s) and methods (one piece of equipment or software application is different from the rest)
- differences between suppliers, customers, products, locations, etc.

A control chart, just like a run chart, is typically constructed by plotting the frequency of an event over a period of time. However, in a control chart we also calculate and display a centre line and process control limits in order to observe, identify and investigate variability in a process. These statistically determined control limits allow us to understand process capability and evaluate improvements (changes) to be made to a process. Determination of control limits requires some statistical knowledge as it depends on the type of data used.

One of the objectives of using control charts is to detect and investigate special causes. A process from which special causes have been removed is said to be stable and in the state of statistical control. Once special causes are detected and removed, the next step is to improve the stabilized process by taking actions on the common causes. Typically, common causes are more difficult to detect and eliminate. Using a Six Sigma project, actions are taken on the common causes and, where required, fundamental changes are made to the process.

There are two important indicators that can be used to identify special causes in a control chart (Figure 3.16). Any point that occurs outside of the control limits is an indication for an unusual situation. Such a point usually indicates that the process is out of control and requires investigation of the root cause. The second indicator is the systematic pattern which some points display. Even if all the points are between the control limits, a systematic occurrence (trend) of points or an unusual pattern indicates that the process may be out of control as it does not behave in a random manner.

Summary

The principal focus of a Six Sigma project is process improvement. Typical Six Sigma projects are classified mainly into 'Black Belt' or 'Green Belt' projects, depending on their duration and/or importance. Quick Shot projects, another type of Six Sigma project, are usually carried out without the need for extensive data collection and analysis.

A typical Six Sigma project is defined by the acronym DMAIC which stands for:

- define
- measure
- analyse
- improve
- control.

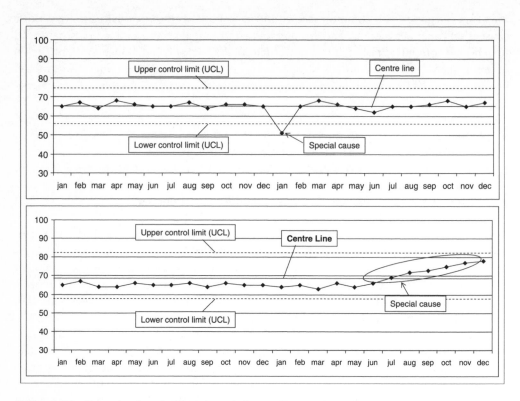

Figure 3.16 Example of a simplified control chart with typical special causes

The define phase identifies any need for improvement and thus the requirements for a project, including project owner, project scope and project leader. VOC and VOB are vital for the selection and prioritization of projects. Tools to assist the define phase include:

- QFD – used to prioritize the CTQs
- the CE chart – used to highlight factors with higher importance.

The measure phase actually measures the process performance and pinpoints problems and other areas requiring improvement. One of the important features of this phase is the collection of data. Tangible or objective measures are called hard data, while less tangible and subjective measures are referred to as the soft data.

Data can be categorized into continuous data, usually obtained through measurement, and discrete data, usually gathered through observations or counts of occurrences. Tools used for this phase include:

- the Pareto chart – used mainly for focusing on a problem, analysing the problems and deciding on improvement targets, and determining the effect of the improvement
- the histogram – used to study the distribution characteristics of a data set
- the run chart – used to depict the occurrence of an event over a specified period of time.

The analyse phase identifies root causes of a problem and/or the critical factors for process improvement. Common tools for this phase include:

- IPO – used to depict the inputs and outputs of a process and how that process is linked to another
- the PF chart – used to identify the activities within a process and how they relate to one another
- the CE chart – used to identify improvement areas or root causes of a problem.

Six Sigma defines process output as metrics. The focus is always on the identification of factors with higher impact (Vital Fews = critical Xs) *versus* various other activities (Trivial Many = Xs) of a process.

The improve phase identifies and implements actions to reduce or eliminate the negative effect of the Vital Fews, or to increase their positive effect on the achievement of an improvement target. Typical tools used for this phase include:

- the FMEA chart – used for the identification of improvement actions
- the Gantt chart – used to plan implementation actions.

The control phase ensures the new process is stable after the implementation of the changes, standardizes those changes and ensures the information about the changes are communicated to all stakeholders. Commonly used tools for this phase include:

- the control chart – used for measuring stability by displaying the trend and pattern of a process
- IPO and PF charts – used to standardize and document the new process.

4 *Six Sigma Teams and Training*

Introduction

As we have discussed, Six Sigma projects are at the heart of the Six Sigma methodology. These projects are carried out by a number of carefully selected and sufficiently trained personnel, who form teams with a Champion and project leader. Most project teams are usually made of an organization's own personnel. However, it is also important to include suppliers and even customers in the Six Sigma projects as needed. Figure 4.1 illustrates a typical Six Sigma infrastructure. This comprises five levels representing several layers of organizational hierarchy. Each Six Sigma level has its own roles, duties and responsibilities.

Six Sigma levels and their roles

EXECUTIVE CHAMPION

The Executive Champion is usually the person who is in charge of the company or business unit. The role of the Executive Champion typically involves the following:

Six Sigma role	Position	Main duties and responsibilities
Executive Champion	CEO/Managing Director	Decision making
Champion	GMs/Directors	Implementation within division
Black Belt	Managers	Project management
Green Belt	Assistant managers	Process improvement
Master Black Belt	Process improvement specialist	Coaching, consulting, training and project support

Figure 4.1 Six Sigma roles and their main duties and responsibilities

- setting company goals and objectives using Six Sigma
- defining the necessary infrastructure for Six Sigma
- identifying and providing resources needed for Six Sigma deployment
- identifying Six Sigma training requirements
- promoting Six Sigma throughout the organization.

CHAMPION

Champions (or project sponsors) play an important role within Six Sigma as they are responsible for the implementation of Six Sigma in their divisions. Some of the common duties of a Champion include:

- aligning project activities with company goals and objectives
- selecting Six Sigma projects
- assigning Black Belts to the projects
- providing consistent guidance and support to project teams
- knocking down barriers where needed
- monitoring progress of the projects (project reviews)
- sharing best practices after the completion of projects
- recognizing project gains and rewarding project members.

BLACK BELT

Black Belts are typically selected from the middle management. Some of the common tasks of this role include:

- managing and facilitating Six Sigma projects
- providing technical support to Champions
- identifying opportunities for improvement
- mentoring Green Belts
- providing guidance and training to team members.

Black Belt selection requires special attention. It is advisable to prepare a list of selection criteria comprising both technical and non-technical skills required for this role. Figure 4.2 shows a list of recommendation criteria which can be used as guidelines for Black Belt selection.

GREEN BELT

Green Belts are usually chosen from the staff levels within a department. It is recommended to use a list of selection criteria (similar to that used in the Black Belt selection process) reflecting the relevant requirements of this role. Green Belts play an important part within Six Sigma as they are directly involved in the execution of the Six Sigma projects. Some of the typical tasks of this role include:

- collecting and analysing process data
- identifying requirements for process changes

Technical requirements	Non-technical requirements
• Project management skills	• Interpersonal skills
• Financial understanding	• Leadership skills
• Workplace knowledge	• Values and behaviours
• Process thinking	• Creative thinking
• Customer skills	• Critical thinking
• Entrepreneurial skills	• Trusted by others
• Statistical thinking	• Respected by others
• Six Sigma knowledge	

Figure 4.2   Recommendations for Black Belt selection

- implementing changes to processes
- monitoring changed or improved processes.

MASTER BLACK BELT

Perhaps one of the most critical roles within Six Sigma is the role of the Master Black Belt. It is a role which not only builds a bridge between the other roles but also coordinates and facilitates all Six Sigma activities within the organization or the business unit. Typical activities and duties of this role include:

- coordinating Six Sigma activities within the organization or business unit
- providing consultancy to Champions and Black Belts
- providing support to project teams
- training Black Belts and Green Belts.

Origins of the Six Sigma teams

The idea of improving the quality of products and services through formal teams is not new. It is widely accepted that the applications of total quality management (TQM) initiatives generated enormous interest in formal team structures in the 1980s and 1990s. During the TQM era, many Western organizations began to use formal teams for tackling problems in all departments and work areas. Staff involvement and problem-solving were the two key ingredients of the TQM initiative. As we discussed in Chapter 1, most TQM organizations used two types of teams: Quality Council and Quality Circle. Both teams were permanent and consisted of several employees. The Quality Council was a cross-functional team, which mainly consisted of members of middle management and was tasked to drive the TQM initiative. Quality Circle was a group of six to eight people selected from departmental staff and tasked with solving quality problems within their own work area.

One of the main differences between Six Sigma and TQM is that Six Sigma teams are not

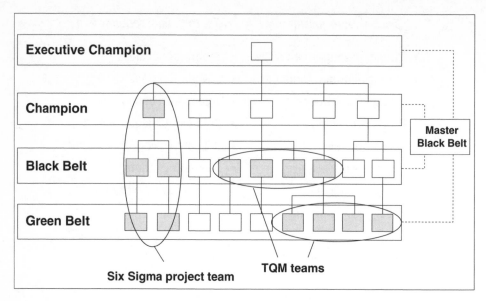

Figure 4.3   Comparison of Six Sigma and TQM teams

permanent and involve at least three different levels of the organizational hierarchy (Figure 4.3). In this context, Six Sigma teams don't replace but complement the TQM teams. Both Six Sigma teams and TQM teams can coexist in an organization if their roles and purposes are clearly defined. For instance, Six Sigma teams are often formed to tackle those problems identified by the senior management while quality circle teams can continue solving problems in their own work area.

Managing the Six Sigma teams

There are three types of Six Sigma projects, depicted in Figure 4.4, that depend on the size and scope of the project. Regardless of type, all Six Sigma projects must have a sponsor or Champion. They must be registered and approved by a Champion. Like other teams, Six Sigma teams also require proper team management activities including planning, coordinating, communicating, motivating, training and support. It is critical to the success of Six Sigma teams that a team charter is prepared before commencing the projects. Things to consider in the team charter may include:

- preparation of a statement of purpose
- selection of team members
- roles and responsibilities of team members
- form and frequency of team meetings
- reporting procedures
- resources needed by the teams
- training needs of team members
- communication rules within the teams
- follow-up review procedures
- closing out procedures.

	Black Belt project	Green Belt project	'Quick Shot' project
Team size	5–8 team members (led by a Black Belt)	3–5 team members (led by a Green Belt)	<3 people
Project scope	Tackling cross-functional and/or complex processes which require extensive data collection and analysis	Analysis and improvement of small and less complex processes, often within the own department or division	Ideas or suggestions for processes improvement which do not require further analysis but must be approved by a Champion
Project duration	3–5 months	1–2 months	<1 month

Figure 4.4   Six Sigma project teams

Project teams should meet on a regular basis – at least once a month – to achieve a smooth progress of the project. The team leader should ensure that:

- meetings are planned ahead
- goals and objectives are clearly identified
- tasks are effectively communicated to the team members
- minutes of the meetings are kept
- support is obtained from the project sponsor (Champion) or Master Black Belt where needed.

Team progress reports are very useful project management tools and should be taken seriously by the team leaders and sponsors. Presenting progress reports to project sponsors at predetermined formal review meetings will ensure that the sponsor has been informed about progress made or problems encountered and the team leader is enabled to collect the sponsor's input for the following steps. To ensure smooth bottom-up communication, the project sponsor should present regular project reports at the executive management meetings.

Six Sigma training

At the start, Six Sigma requires a certain amount of investment in education and training. Some organizations, for instance General Electric, have spent millions of dollars in training their thousands of Black Belts and ten thousands of Green Belts. Before commencing training sessions, top management should ensure that Six Sigma is clearly communicated to all levels. People in the organization usually find out quickly if a new management initiative is being rolled out. A lot of misperceptions or misinterpretations can be avoided if some generic information is distributed to all members of staff. This can be achieved through publication of statements in company newspapers or using the intranet, plus verbal statements in various staff meetings, forums and events.

It is the responsibility of the top management to identify what training is required. Not everyone needs heavy statistics in order to carry out a Six Sigma project. A sound training programme starts with the identification of the training needs for various Six Sigma levels. As discussed in the previous chapters, processes in transactional and service environments differ in many ways from manufacturing processes. The second important thing to consider is the state of the Six Sigma deployment. At the early stage, only a few people are trained to kick off the Six Sigma initiative. At this stage, an understanding of the concept and some basic tools are more important than applying advanced statistical knowledge to the projects. Many organizations call this early stage the 'early gains' or 'reaping the low-hanging fruit'. As organizations mature with the Six Sigma concept, more people are selected for Black Belt or Green Belt training and there may also be an increasing need for some people to be trained in advanced statistics.

Some of the commonly asked questions about the various Belts refer to the activities performed by these Belts and may include:

- How many Black Belts and how many Green Belts does my company need?
- Is it better to have Belts on a full-time or part-time basis?
- Is there a difference between a manufacturing Belt and a transactional Belt?
- Like many other companies, do we also need Yellow and White Belts?
- How long does it take to certify the various Belts?

All these questions should be identified and answered before commencing the training programme. Most of these questions touch on multiple aspects. For instance, let's take a look at the question 'How many Black Belts and how many Green Belts does an organization need?' This will mainly depend on the scope of the deployment programme. Many organizations start their Six Sigma programme with a small number of employees and in some sections of the business only, before expanding it to other areas of the business. Sony, for instance, started the implementation of Six Sigma in its manufacturing plants and predominantly in Japan. This first step took around three years. Later, Sony decided to roll out Six Sigma to the transactional side of the businesses and deploy it in every part of the world to all their organizations. The second step is believed to have taken another three or four years. In one of the Sony transactional operations in Australia, for instance, the roll out process took more than one year and only 10 per cent of the total staff were trained in Six Sigma. Whether in manufacturing or transactional businesses, the number of Six Sigma teams will always be a matter of what your company needs.

There are several advantages and disadvantages of having full-time operating Belts. No doubt, one of the main benefits is that full-time Black or Green Belts will focus on the process improvements, which *may* result in substantial savings. This is a quick solution to the problem and may produce good short-term returns on investment. On the other hand, having full-time 'cost reduction experts' may cause disturbances within the organization. Many people are resistant to 'external' experts and may feel threatened by them. The risk of losing an expert to your competition or someone else, is also high considering the attractive salaries being offered by some companies in the USA and elsewhere for skilled Six Sigma practitioners. One of the benefits of having part-time Belts is that more people can be trained and involved in the Six Sigma initiative. This may generate a cultural push towards better results, which are mid- or long-term rather than short-term results.

Many practitioners argue that there should be two types of Black and Green Belts: the manufacturing Belts and the transactional Belts. It is difficult to follow this argument if one considers that both manufacturing and the non-manufacturing Belts have the same role. That is, to improve process by carrying out a project. Most of the basic Six Sigma tools used in manufacturing processes are no different from the transactional and service processes. The underlying concept and philosophy is also the same. What might be different is the application to a particular problem. What tools to use will mainly depend on the complexity of the problem. It is very difficult to understand why manufacturing processes are inherently more complex than transactional or service processes. Straightforward and more complex processes exist in all types of work environments.

Although this is not a common practice, some large companies use Yellow Belts and White Belts to train new employees or other personnel with limited process knowledge. These training sessions are mainly used to introduce those employees to Six Sigma concepts. In some organizations, for instance, new employees undergo a White Belt training while more experienced staff are offered a Yellow Belt training course. The duration and scope of the White Belt and Yellow Belt training courses vary from company to company. In general, two to four hours of White Belt training should be sufficient to explain the basics of Six Sigma, while Yellow Belt training may be conducted over one or two days.

As we described in the previous chapters, Six Sigma works best if it is applied as a top-down approach. Therefore, the training programme should begin with the executive management level (Executive Champion). The main objective of the Executive Champion is to develop an understanding of the Six Sigma concept and its underlying philosophy, and to start developing strategies for the Six Sigma deployment throughout the organization. The next training level is the senior management or general management level (Champion). During the Champion training, the participants learn how to implement Six Sigma within their own divisions or departments. They also learn how to select Black Belt projects and how to direct and support the project teams.

The next step in the training process is the middle management and other key personnel who are trained as Black Belts. Six Sigma experts' opinion is divided about the length and content of Black Belt training. Many organizations, for instance, provide up to four weeks' training which usually contains a considerable quantity of advanced statistics. Other organizations, on the other hand, use a condensed Black Belt curriculum of five or six days and then later offer advanced statistics training separately to selected Black Belts for whom it is appropriate (see Figure 4.5). In the latter case, this not only reduces costs dramatically but also provide statistics training to only those who really need it. During the training, Black Belts are asked to solve a particular project in order to qualify for certification. This certification is renewed every two or three years depending on the company's re-certification guidelines.

As with the Black Belts, Green Belt training can be conducted by using two different curricula: the longer version, which includes some advanced statistics and takes two to three weeks to complete, and the condensed version, which is only three or four days long and contains only basic statistics in the curriculum. Whichever versions a company may choose, one of the fundamental differences between the Black Belt and the Green Belt training curriculum is that Black Belts usually focus on how to manage Six Sigma projects while Green Belts are more concerned about measuring processes, and the identification and implementation of improvement actions.

Six Sigma role	Training duration	Training content
Executive Champion	1 day	Six Sigma overview
Champion	2 days	Six Sigma overview; Six Sigma deployment; Project selection
Black Belt	5–6 days	Selection and management of Six Sigma projects
Green Belt	3–4 days	Process analysis and improvement
Master Black Belt	4–5 weeks	Deployment and use of Six Sigma concept; Advanced statistical tools; Coaching and training methods

Figure 4.5   Six Sigma training

Certifying the Six Sigma Belts

Certification requirements of the various Belts differ from organization to organization. Many companies issue a certificate of attendance after completion of Belt training sessions. During the training, employees are asked to solve a workplace problem in the form of a project. The certificate of attendance is usually a confirmation that participants have demonstrated the necessary competency to apply their learned skills to the real-world situations. It does not guarantee that they will be performing well in the following months and years. Therefore, a regular surveillance of the Belt activities is crucial to the successful implementation of the Six Sigma programme. Some organizations conduct a final certification review after two or three years and issue a licence to the successful candidates. Poorly performing Belts are either given another chance to qualify or lose their qualification status.

Rewarding the Six Sigma teams

One of the frequently asked questions refers to the recognition and reward mechanisms for the various Belts. Again, there are no common rules, which can be applied by all companies. It is widely accepted that monetary rewards may provide some incentives and motivation to achieve better results. However, many organizations believe monetary reward mechanisms are difficult to manage and may generate only short-term motivation. Nowadays, it is quite common that process improvement is a mandatory position requirement for senior and middle management. In some companies, for instance, process improvement has been made mandatory and included in the descriptions of positions in senior and middle management, linking their annual performance bonuses directly to the degree of their involvement in the Six Sigma programme. Beside the many other factors, the successful completion of Six Sigma projects is a major contributor to their performance bonuses.

Summary

A Six Sigma infrastructure is composed of five layers ranging from the Executive Champion (usually the CEO/managing director) through Champions (heads of divisions), Black Belts (managers) and Green Belts (assistant managers), to the Master Black Belt (a process improvement specialist).

The Executive Champion's principal responsibility involves high-level decision-making during the Six Sigma deployment process. This may include defining infrastructure and training requirements, providing resources and promoting Six Sigma. Champions are responsible for the implementation of Six Sigma within their divisions and the alignment of Six Sigma projects with organizational goals and objectives. Black Belt activities typically include management of the Six Sigma projects and mentoring Green Belts. The selection of a Black Belt candidate requires care and should be performed using a set of technical and non-technical requirements suitable for this role. Green Belts' main activities include measuring process and identifying and implementing improvement actions. A Master Black Belt coordinates and facilitates all Six Sigma activities within a discrete business unit or the entire company, and provides consultancy and support when needed.

Unlike those in TQM, Six Sigma teams are vertical and non-permanent. They involve personnel from three different levels of organizational hierarchy: Champion, Black Belt and Green Belt. Where needed, TQM and Six Sigma teams can complement each other.

Six Sigma projects can be classified into three types: Black Belt projects, Green Belt projects, and Quick Shot projects. The main differentiating factors between these projects are complexity, duration and size. Black Belt and Green Belt projects must have a Champion and project leader. Project teams *must* meet regularly; this depends on their size, but it must be at least once a month. They must also have a project charter. Quick Shot projects are usually small in scale and can be carried out without extensive data analysis. However, they are also registered and reviewed as Six Sigma projects. All projects should report using progress reports. In turn, the project Champion/sponsor provides progress reports to the executive management.

All Six Sigma teams must be trained. It is the responsibility of top management to identify what training is required and at what levels, including the number of Black Belt and Green Belts the company needs or requires. The implementation of Six Sigma should start modestly with a few individuals being trained to produce immediate benefits and then expanding over time to the predetermined full complement. Some large organizations also use Yellow and White Belts. Generally these are entities with limited process skill, but they gain valuable process experience and provide a process focus within the bulk of the workforce.

The key feature of Six Sigma is its top-down management approach. Training in an implementing organization should start with the executive management, to develop the Six Sigma concepts and philosophy, and then continue on down through Master Black Belts, Black Belts, Green Belts, and finally the optional Yellow/White Belts. The recommended implementation of Six Sigma is an evolving process and means that the top-down approach can be implemented in a series of slices until the full implementation is achieved.

There is a variety of training methods and practices, discussed in this chapter, which are mainly tailored to suit the implementing organization. The lack of prescription-type requirements in training methods and usage of various tools and techniques is the flexibility of the Six Sigma methodology, which makes it attractive to potential implementing organizations.

After training, certification of trained Belts needs to be addressed. Currently, there is no standardized and nationally or internationally accepted certification scheme available. Many universities and commercially oriented training organizations provide training courses and certifications; however, none of them is widely recognized. Large organizations, like General Electric and Sony, developed their own in-house training and certification guidelines to suit their organizational cultures and preferences.

It is important that all performing Belt levels are suitably rewarded. This may be achieved through recognition, re-certification, promotion and/or monetary rewards such as bonuses and salary increases. Whatever the form, the principal reward is after the successful completion of a Six Sigma project.

5 *Six Sigma Toolbox*

Introduction

The Six Sigma methodology uses an extensive array of process analysis and improvement methods and practices. These are called Six Sigma tools. Most of the tools are not new and were developed in the past five decades. However, the way some of the tools are applied within the Six Sigma methodology differs from their traditional use.

When implementing Six Sigma, it is important to differentiate between two sets of tools and techniques:

- basic or common tools and techniques and
- advanced tools which are used where needed, and only where appropriate.

As mentioned in the earlier chapters, the purpose of this book is to focus on the application of Six Sigma, not on the tools themselves. It is the author's opinion that most improvement projects in transactional and service environments can be carried out by using basic tools and techniques. Even in manufacturing environments, there are relatively few projects which require more advanced (statistical) tools.

The tools and techniques used in this book include:

- Pareto charts or diagrams
- histograms
- process capability indices *Cp* and *Cpk*
- measurement system analysis (MSA)
- control charts
- input-process-output (IPO) models
- process flow (PF) charts
- cross-functional (CF) process maps
- cause-and-effect (CE) charts
- tree diagrams
- quality function deployment (QFD) charts
- failure-mode-effect-analysis (FMEA) charts
- Gantt charts.

Throughout the book, these tools have been discussed by using specific examples of their application. In this chapter, we focus on how some of these tools are constructed or conducted. These include:

- constructing Pareto charts

- constructing histograms
- calculating process capability indices *Cp* and *Cpk*
- conducting an MSA
- constructing control charts.

Constructing a Pareto chart

A Pareto chart is often used to rank data groups or classes in a descending or ascending order in order to separate critical factors from less important ones. In a way, it is a prioritization tool. It is simple to construct and provides a sound foundation for decision-making.

There are two steps in constructing a Pareto chart:

- preparing data for charting and
- plotting the chart.

The first step is grouping data in categories, ranking the categories and calculating absolute and cumulative percentages for each category. In Figure 5.1, for instance, the sales volume for a given period of time has been grouped in product categories and ranked from the highest sales volume at the top to the lowest at the bottom. The percentage of sales volume for all categories has been calculated and entered into the third column. The cumulative percentage has been obtained by adding up percentages of the categories. For instance, the second category (22.0 per cent) has been added to the first (30.8 per cent) and the result (52.8 per cent) entered in the last column.

Product category	Sales volume ($)	Sales volume (%)	Sales volume cumulative (%)
TV	1 200 000	30.8	30.8
VCR	860 000	22.0	52.8
DVD	600 000	15.4	68.2
Video camera	400 000	10.3	78.5
Still camera	280 000	7.2	85.7
Home audio	180 000	4.6	90.3
Home projector	110 000	2.8	93.1
Car audio	100 000	2.6	95.7
Recording media	80 000	2.0	97.7
PC	60 000	1.5	99.2
PDA	30 000	0.8	100.0
Total	**3 900 000**	**100%**	

Figure 5.1   Example of data grouped in categories to construct a Pareto chart

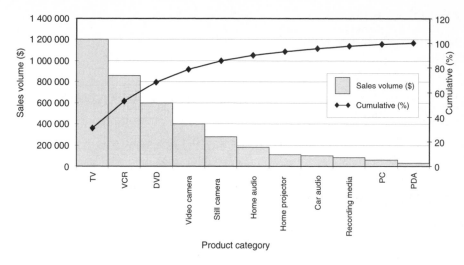

Figure 5.2 Example of a Pareto chart which has been plotted using MS Excel XP for the data shown in Figure 5.1

The second step is plotting the chart. Figure 5.2 illustrates the Pareto chart which has been plotted using MS Excel XP for the data as shown in Figure 5.1. Pareto charts assist in identifying the factors of higher importance. This is demonstrated by the 80/20 rule we discussed in Chapter 3. In general, 80 per cent of results are produced by 20 per cent of inputs. In the example illustrated in Figure 5.2, the first four product categories (TV, VCR, DVD and video camera) contribute to 80 per cent of the company's total sales.

Constructing a histogram

Frequency plots are often used to study the frequency (occurrence) characteristics of a data set. For this purpose, observations are arranged in such a way that they can be conveniently plotted over numerically ordered classes or categories. Frequency plots show the distribution of a data set, thus enabling us to study and compare the characteristics of various distributions. One of the most commonly used frequency plots is the histogram where individual data values are plotted as a bar.

When constructing a histogram, it is important to establish the appropriate classes or categories as the first step. A typical problem associated with the selection of classes is that if the number and width of classes are not suitable, overlapping of the classes may occur. It is then advisable to select the desired number of classes before determining the width of class intervals. The common rule here is to select a number between 5 and 15. To determine the width of the class intervals, the entire range of data is divided by the number of desired classes:

$$\text{Width of class interval} = \frac{\text{Range}}{\text{Number of classes}}$$

In the following example, construction of a histogram ('Distribution of bun weight') has been demonstrated by using a simple four-step procedure:

STEP 1: COLLECT THE DATA

Number of observations (n) = 32
    See Figure 5.3.

STEP 2: DETERMINE THE WIDTH OF CLASS INTERVAL AND ARRANGE THE DATA ACCORDINGLY

Range = 130–120 = 10, desired number of classes = 10, Class width = 1.
    See Figure 5.4.

STEP 3: DISPLAY THE DISTRIBUTION

See Figure 5.5.

120	125	128	127	124	125	128	122
123	121	123	126	126	127	130	123
124	125	125	121	128	129	127	129
126	124	122	127	125	126	124	122

Figure 5.3 Measurement of bun weight in grams

Class interval	120	121	122	123	124	125	126	127	128	129	130
Occurrence	1	2	3	3	4	5	4	4	3	2	1

Figure 5.4 Bun weight classes and their frequencies

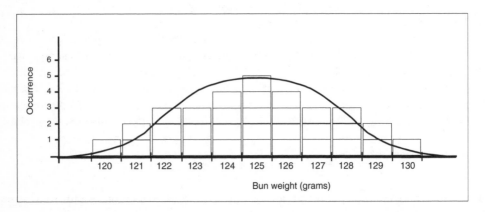

Figure 5.5 Distribution of bun weight

STEP 4: DETERMINE THE DISTRIBUTION CHARACTERISTICS LOCATION (MEAN) AND SPREAD (STANDARD DEVIATION)

Average (bun weight): $\bar{X} = \dfrac{\Sigma X_i}{n} = 250.06$ grams

Standard deviation (bun weight): $S = \sqrt{\dfrac{\Sigma (X_i - \bar{X})^2}{n - 1}} = 2.56$ grams

Calculating the process capability indices *Cp* and *Cpk*

One of the objectives of determining the distribution characteristics 'average' and 'standard deviation' is that they allow us to analyse and understand the variation in a process and whether the process is capable of achieving specified requirements. Before measuring process capability, it is necessary to ensure the process is in a state of statistical control. 'Process capability' is not to be confused with 'process control', which is discussed in the section 'Constructing a control chart' at the end of this chapter. A simple method of obtaining information about process capability is to compare the specified requirements (in other words: what customers want) with the actual variation in the process. Process variation is typically measured by the standard deviation (σ or s). Specification requirements are often referred to as the 'engineering tolerance' which is expressed by upper specification limit (USL) and lower specification limit (LSL).

Process capability index *Cp*: $Cp = \dfrac{\text{USL} - \text{LSL}}{6 \times \sigma}$

Process Capability Index *Cp* uses $6 \times \sigma$ (six times sigma) as process variation (often referred to as the 'natural tolerance') and makes a direct comparison with the engineering tolerance under the assumption that process mean (average) is exactly in the centre of the engineering tolerance.

Figure 5.6 illustrates the *Cp* index of a process in three different stages. A process with a *Cp* index of less than 1.00 is considered as not 'capable' of meeting specified requirements. The *Cp* index is a simple way of obtaining valuable information about process capability. However, it does not consider any shift of process mean that usually occurs in almost every process over time.

The use of the *Cpk* index for process capability analysis is more sensitive as it considers process shifts. The *Cpk* index is defined as:

For two-sided specifications: $C_{pk} = \text{minimum} \left(\dfrac{\text{USL} - \mu}{3 \times \sigma}, \dfrac{\mu - \text{LSL}}{3 \times \sigma} \right)$

For one-sided specifications:

(a) Upper specification limit: $C_{pk} = \dfrac{\text{USL} - \mu}{3 \times \sigma}$

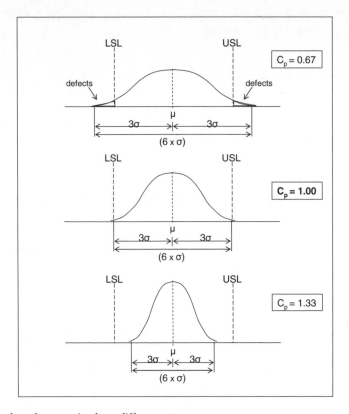

Figure 5.6   *Cp* index of process in three different stages

(b) Lower specification limit: $C_{pk} = \dfrac{\mu - LSL}{3 \times \sigma}$

Figure 5.7 illustrates the comparison of *Cp* and *Cpk* indices for the same process. In Panel A, process average is centred, thus the numeric values for the *Cp* index and the *Cpk* index are the same. However, when process mean shifts to one side (Panel B), the *Cp* index is not able to capture the effect of the shift due to comparison of the total tolerances.

Conducting a measurement system analysis

The aim of measurement system analysis (MSA) is to validate the collected information. A typical measurement system consists of three components: a measurement device, a method of measurement and an entity who carries out the measurement. The suitability of the measurement instrument, its precision and calibration are some of the typical errors associated with the measurement device. Measurement method related errors may include an incorrect sampling procedure and inaccurate instructions. Insufficient training and lack of attention by the operator taking the measures are just two of the common errors that may occur due to human factors.

'Accuracy' is the distance of the average of measurement values from a known standard value. Measurements are 'repeatable' and 'stable' when the same person always obtains the

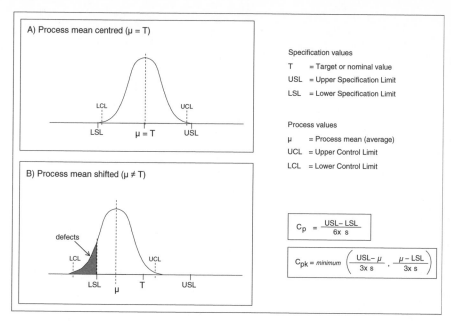

Figure 5.7 Comparison of *CP* and *Cpk* indices for the same process with and without process mean shift

same result over time. In other words, the less variation we get, the more repeatable is the measurement. 'Reproducibility' is the result of measuring one characteristic by different entities. If the difference of the average of the observed values is large, the measurement is said to be less reproducible. See Figure 5.8 for an illustration of these definitions.

Constructing a control chart

It is widely accepted that statistical quality control began with Walter Shewhart of Bell Telephone Laboratories, who developed and used a statistical chart for control of product variables in 1924. During the past 80 years many industries, including aeronautics, car and electronics manufacturing, have made extensive use of statistical control charts to understand, control and improve their processes. Control charts enable us to monitor a process and detect statistically significant process changes before they cause unwanted defects. This technique is often called 'statistical process control' (SPC).

Like run charts, control charts also display data over time. However, unlike a run chart that is mainly used to show trends, a control chart not only allows us to detect significant trends but also assists in studying process variability. Sources of process variability can be divided into two main categories: the common causes and the special causes.

Common causes of process variability are typically inherent to the process and have random occurrences, while special causes follow an unusual pattern in their occurrence (with a sporadic or occasional appearance) and often have relatively large impact on the process. Control charts are commonly used in both manufacturing and non-manufacturing environments. There are two different types of control chart: the control chart for variables and the control chart for attributes.

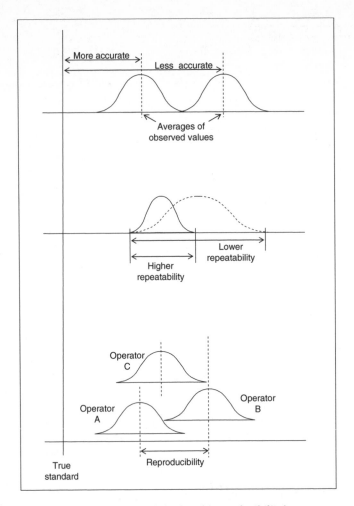

Figure 5.8   Illustration of 'accuracy', 'repeatability' and 'reproducibility'

Control charts for variables can be broken down two main groups:

- control charts for individual data (X charts)
- control charts for grouped data (X bar charts).

One of the most commonly used control charts for grouped data is the X bar and range (R) chart (Figure 5.9). In order to use the X bar and R chart, it is actually necessary to construct two different charts: the X bar chart, which displays the average of a sample or subgroup, and the R chart, which plots the range of the sample or subgroup. When using the X bar and R chart, we should take the following into consideration:

- the determination of the quality characteristic and time span to be examined
- the determination of the sampling plan (sample size, method of sampling, and so on).

Once the collected data have been validated as reliable, relevant and representative of the

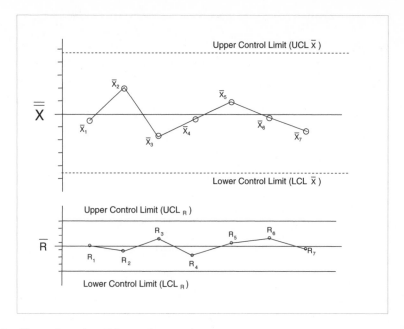

Figure 5.9   Illustration of an X bar and range chart

process outputs, the calculation of the sample average, range, centre line and control limits can be performed using the equations in Figure 5.10.

Figure 5.11 shows values for the constants A_2, D_3 and D_4 to be used when calculating the control limits for the X bar and R charts.

Control charts for attributes can be broken down into two main groups:

- control charts for defects or nonconformities in units (c and u control charts)
- control charts for defectives or nonconforming units (p and pn control charts).

C and u control charts are used when we count the number of defects (occurrences) per unit (intervals or areas of observation). For instance, we want to count the number of errors on invoices every month. If we examine the same number of invoices and count the errors found on them every month, then we use the c chart. If the number of invoices examined every month is different, then the u chart will be more appropriate.

P and pn control charts are used to count the number of defective items (for instance, products or transactions) sampled from a process. 'Defective' means not meeting the specified requirements. A pn chart displays the number of defectives per sample and may be used only if the sample size is constant. The p chart shows a plot of the proportion defectives per sample and can be used for constant sample size as well as for varying sample size. The proportion can be expressed as a fraction or percentage.

Summary

Six Sigma uses a variety of methods and practices for the analysis and improvement of

Sample average:	$\overline{X} = \dfrac{X_1 + X_2 + ... + X_k}{n}$	n = Sample size $\overline{X}$ = Average of sample or subgroup $X_1 + X_2 + ... + X_k$ = Individual measurement values
Sample range:	$R = X_{max} - X_{min}$	X_{max} = Highest value in sample or subgroup X_{min} = Lowest value in sample or subgroup
Process average:	$\overline{\overline{X}} = \dfrac{\overline{X}_1 + \overline{X}_2 + ... + \overline{X}_k}{m}$	m = Total number of subgroups $\overline{\overline{X}}$ = Centre line for X bar chart (process average) $\overline{X}_1 + \overline{X}_2 + ... + \overline{X}_k$ = Average of each subgroup
Range centre line:	$\overline{R} = \dfrac{R_1 + R_2 + ... + R_k}{m}$	m = Total number of subgroups $\overline{R}$ = Average of all subgroups $R_1 + R_2 + ... + R_k$ = Range of each subgroup
Process control limits:	$UCL_{\overline{X}} = \overline{\overline{X}} + A_2 \overline{R}$ $LCL_{\overline{X}} = \overline{\overline{X}} - A_2 \overline{R}$	A_2 = Constant (Table 3) $UCL_{\overline{X}}$ = Upper control limit for the X bar chart $LCL_{\overline{X}}$ = Lower control limit for the X bar chart
Range control limits:	$UCL_{\overline{R}} = D_4 \overline{R}$ $LCL_{\overline{R}} = D_3 \overline{R}$	D_3 and D_4 = Constants (Table 3) $UCL_{\overline{R}}$ = Upper control limit for the R chart $LCL_{\overline{R}}$ = Lower control limit for the R chart

Figure 5.10   Equations to be used when constructing X bar and R charts

Subgroup size (n)	A_2	D_3	D_4
4	0.729	0	2.282
5	0.577	0	2.114
6	0.483	0	2.004
7	0.419	0.076	1.924
8	0.373	0.136	1.864
9	0.337	0.184	1.816
10	0.308	0.223	1.777

Figure 5.11   Constants to be used when constructing X bar and R charts

processes. These are called 'Six Sigma tools' and are contained within a feature called the Six Sigma toolbox.

Six Sigma tools are divided into two sets:

- common and
- advanced.

Within the transactional and service environment, common tools are very necessary. It is rare for advanced tools to be employed for those environments – even manufacturing. There is a subset of the common tools, which includes:

- Pareto charts – used primarily to rank data classes, so as to separate critical factors from less important ones. The Pareto chart is considered to be a prioritization tool as well
- histograms – used primarily to examine the distribution characteristics of data. Data are organized into numerically ordered classes or categories
- process capability indices – Cp and Cpk – used primarily to analyse and understand the capability of a process of achieving its requirements
- measurement system analysis (MSA) – used primarily to validate collected information or data. MSA is a defined set of activities which may involve different methods of measurements
- control charts – used primarily to detect and study process variability. Sources of process variability are classified into two categories: common causes and special causes.

Case Studies: Applying Six Sigma to Transactional and Service Environments

Pursuing Customer Service Excellence

Mr Derek Horner
Sony Australia, Australia

Introduction

In 2001–02, Sony Australia implemented the Six Sigma methodology as a corporate initiative driven by Sony headquarters in Japan. This case study is not about how Sony Australia has deployed the Six Sigma methodology within the organization; it is about the application of Six Sigma to typical customer service processes to drive the company's pursuit of customer service excellence.

In pursuit of the unimaginable – a story of vision and invention

In a burnt-out department store in Tokyo in 1946, just after World War II, Masaru Ibuka and Akio Morita, running a company known at the time as Tokyo Tsushin Kogyo (Tokyo Telecommunications Engineering), attempted to produce a simple electric rice cooker. It didn't work too well – but so began their desire to produce products for everyday life.

In 1958, the company name was changed to the Sony Corporation and, since that time, Sony has become one of the most recognized brand names in the history of the modern world. Sony – derived from the Latin word *sonus*, which means sound; coupled with the English term 'sonny' referring to young boys of the 1950s – was chosen because it was simple, easy to read and could be pronounced in any language.

The Sony Corporation now spans a range of industries which includes audiovisual electronics, information technology, broadcasting, telecommunications, entertainment, satellite broadcasting and insurance/finance. Sony has almost 1000 consolidated subsidiaries, more than 168 000 employees worldwide and, in the fiscal year ending March 2002, sales hit a record US$57 billion.

From the world's first transistor radio in 1955, the Trinitron colour television, Walkman, Betacam, compact disc, Wega and memory stick, Sony has continually made things smaller and smarter, and displayed more innovation, than was ever thought possible – constantly challenging the creativity of Sony's customers. Throughout the world, Sony stands for innovation, state-of-the-art technology and superior quality. Sony's vision over its next fifty years is to offer people exciting new products and new lifestyles and the corporation is committed to the challenge of creating and realizing these dreams.

Sony Australia Limited

Sony began its operations in Australia in 1962, and the corporation currently employs over 300 employees nationally. Its core business is the distribution of electronic products to consumers and industry. The product range is divided into three main areas:

(a)   consumer products
(b)   broadcast and professional products and
(c)   information technology products.

Sony's key stakeholders

Sony Australia's key stakeholders are retail partners, distributors, dealers, customers, local and national community and government organizations. They can be defined in detail as follows:

- *Customers* – purchasers of Sony products and users of Sony services
- *Media* – reporting on technology trends, consumer feedback and the market performance of Sony Australia
- *Employees* – interested in job satisfaction, a quality workplace, occupational health and safety (OH&S) regulations and career progress
- *Retail partners* – interested in new products, supply stability and technology
- *Contractor and suppliers* – interested in opportunities within Sony Australia on specific projects. A quality controlled workplace environment and OH&S regulation are important factors
- *Competitors* – producing comparative products
- *Community* – interested in Sony Australia's environmental initiatives, safety controls, sponsorship and philanthropic issues
- Investors – interested in Sony Corporation's performance and require sound business decisions to enhance Sony's reputation as a leading multinational company.

Management systems

Sony Australia's management team has developed and implemented strict policies relating to the Quality Management System (QMS), Environmental Management System (EMS), Compliance Management System (CMS) and Safety Management System (SMS), as well as the Personal Information Management (PIM) and Customer Service Management (CSM) systems. The corporation is committed to honesty and integrity and ensures that all members of staff comply with Sony Australia's code of conduct.

Sony Australia has adopted the Sony Quality Policy following the guidelines of the Australian and New Zealand Standards for a Quality Management System, AS/NZS 9001:2000 (www.iso.ch). Sony continually reviews its quality management systems to ensure all associated programmes meet customers' expectations efficiently and effectively.

Sony's commitment to customer service

Sony's reputation for developing and manufacturing quality products is backed up by quality after-sales service. The delivery of product innovation and product quality does not guarantee success in the market; Sony must provide high levels of customer service to complete the package to the customer. To facilitate this, Sony Australia's customer service division (CSD) consists of four main departments (Figure CS.1a):

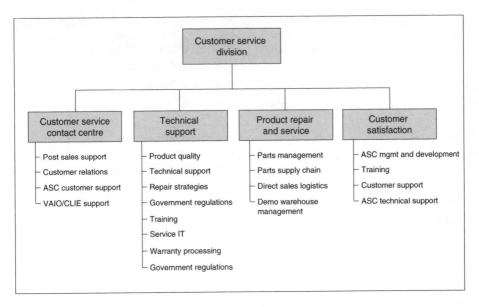

Figure CS.1a   Customer service division organizational structure

- Customer service contact centre
- Product technical support
- Product repair and service (spare parts)
- Customer satisfaction (see Figure CS.1a).

One of the key functions of the CSD is to engage and manage around 150 authorized service centres (ASCs) to serve Sony customers throughout Australia. Most of these ASCs are independently owned sole traders who are authorized to repair Sony products. Historically, Sony Australia has utilized the services of ASCs because they can provide a 'local' service to customers. The majority of Sony ASCs also repair products for other manufacturers (multi-vendors). Some of the major ASCs, mainly located in capital cities, repair Sony products only. These are known as 'Sony- only ASCs' and have a much closer relationship with Sony Australia than do other ASCs.

In 1995 Sony Australia embarked on a campaign to improve the network of ASCs both in terms of their repair performance and in terms of the quality of their customer service delivery. Part of the campaign was to reduce the overall number of ASCs so that Sony can more efficiently administer and manage them. This has had the effect of concentrating product repairs into the ASCs who were retained on the basis of their commitment to quality.

All ASCs were linked to Sony via the Web using a system called Servman to speed up data transfer, such as parts orders, warranty claims and technical information. This system gives the ASCs real-time access to Sony information systems and services around the clock. Servman has been a valuable tool in improving the overall turnaround time of repairs as it gives the repair technician immediate access to service information (see Figure CS.1b).

What do Sony customers want?

In 2000, Sony Australia carried out a customer survey to study the ASCs' service performance and found out that the majority of the ASCs did not have any

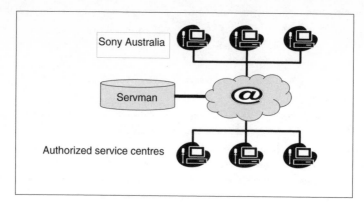

Figure CS.1b   Web-based communication and data transfer over the system Servman

systematic means to deliver consistent customer service. Their methodology was *ad hoc* and fitted each customer event as it occurred. The study revealed that the definition and quality of customer service varied from ASC to ASC. It was found that most ASCs, being part of the 'brown goods' industry, did not have or were not aware of customer service standards.

After further analysis within a three-month period following the survey, it was confirmed that those ASCs who had some form of service guidelines were those who maintained the higher scores for customer service delivery. The survey also revealed that customer communication was an area of particular concern as customers believed that the ASCs' communication performance was below their expectations.

Some of the customer comments gathered from the survey included:

'Took too long.'
'Very poor people skills.'
'Can't even get my name right.'
'Careless attitude.'
'Reception staff was very affronting.'
'No real explanation was given regarding the fault.'
'I had to ring to see if it was ready.'
'The item was in the shop for one

month. In that time I didn't receive any calls notifying me of what was happening with the repair and when I did ring their phone personnel were rude and unhelpful.'

'Staff were pompous – did not explain fault or correction – unconcerned that I had to go back twice. Told me VCR fault was fixed on two occasions when it had not been fixed. Staff attitude was apathetic and uninterested.'

'The service centre "forgot" to call and advise that the unit was ready for collection. The receptionist was quite rude. I had to wait for 15 minutes to be attended to.'

'Generally I was not kept informed of the progress (or lack of). I was, however, happy with the quality of the repair.'

It was understood that communication with customers was a vital part of the repair and service operations. Customers wanted to know whether their repair was going to be delayed and they wanted to know the reason for that. Delays in repair could result from a part on back order, technical problems or other issues. Customers do not like to be 'out of the repair loop' and felt frustrated and upset when they were not treated as important people who expected to be kept informed.

Other forms of communication complaints came from customers who were also concerned about the way some ASCs spoke to them, either in person or on the telephone. In many cases, ASCs did not provide the customer with the greetings expected. Customers did not feel that the ASC staff were empathetic or had an understanding of the difficulties for the customers caused by the product. One of the key findings of the survey was that ASC communications, from the simple skill of answering the telephone to communicating with the customer and keeping them updated with their repair status, varied in many ways.

Benchmarking with other industries

After studying other industries, it was found that service standards were common across some industry sectors, especially in the auto repair and hospitality industries. Each one of their customer service processes were broken down and a standard was adopted. These standards were then drawn up into a guideline and released to all customer service staff. The standards became the core values of the organization and all members of staff were expected to follow them. Staff were trained and measured via the standards, which resulted in consistent customer service delivery.

These findings became the catalyst for the introduction of Sony Australia's own ASC Customer Service Standards. However, the challenge for Sony was how to introduce the standards into the network of ASCs which are, after all, independently owned businesses. To complete the project a thorough analysis was needed to determine the correct processes required. The Six Sigma approach was therefore used as the vehicle to assist Sony Australia in introducing customer service standards to its ASC network.

Developing the Customer Service Standards

Six Sigma is a methodology, which follows a systematic approach to improving processes. In 2000, Sony Corporation made the implementation of Six Sigma in all its operations one of its core strategic objectives. As part of this strategy, the Six Sigma methodology was utilized successfully to plan and implement the Customer Service (CS) Standards Project.

In summary, a project methodology consisting of the following five steps: Define, Measure, Analyse, Improve and Control (DMAIC) was used to guide the Six Sigma:

- Define – what do the customers really want and how do they relate to the company's goals and objectives
- Measure – understand the current process status and set measures of performance
- Analyse – clarify those factors that have greater impact on results and those that don't
- Improve – implement actions to improve critical factors
- Control – establish a control system for each factor and make it a routine function.

It was important that the CS Standards Project was linked with the values and goals of the company, as set by the managing director in the annual Business CE Chart. Sony Australia's organizational goals (which in turn were guided from and linked to Sony Corporation's strategic goals and objectives as set out in the Corporate CE Charts) covered all functional areas within the company including those areas that needed improvement. Utilizing the Business CE Chart, each division within the company took ownership of the corporate projects and then developed Divisional CE Charts to break down the corporate projects to departmental-level projects. The CS Standards Project was derived from the general business goal of 'improve customer satisfaction'. To achieve this goal, a number of projects were realized which dealt with this subject, all relating to various aspects of the improvement of customer relationships, directly or indirectly.

Another aspect of the Define phase was to ensure that all stakeholders were confirmed, that the project was worthy and that its charter accurately documented. Figures CS.1c and CS.1d illustrate the tools and methods used to identify key stakeholders and their requirements, also referred to as the voice of the customer (VOC).

Once confirmed by ASCs and internal departments, the project was then checked against other company priorities to validate and confirm its importance. A QFD (quality-function-deployment) chart was utilized for this task; it listed all future projects and their level of importance. It was found that the CS Standards Project, when compared to other projects, had the highest priority.

At this point, a Six Sigma team was formed comprising of seven members: personnel from the customer satisfaction department and ASCs. The CS Standards Project was then officially assigned to a freshly trained Black Belt and registered a Six Sigma project within the CSD. One of the first team activities was to map the process. Figure CS.1e illustrates a simple process flow (PF) chart which demonstrates how the repair cycle can fail, especially if the customer is not updated about the repair status.

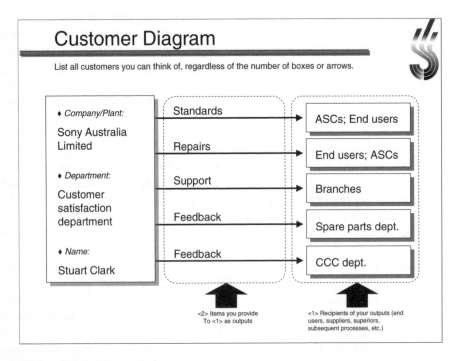

Figure CS.1c　Stakeholders analysis

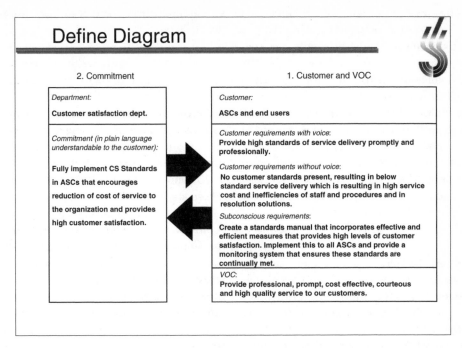

Figure CS.1d   Identifying the 'voice of the customer'

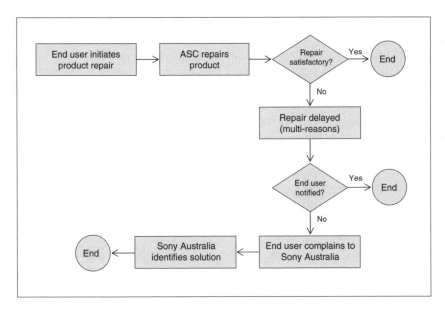

Figure CS.1e   Simple process flow chart illustrating how customer service can fail

During the measure and analyse phases, the causes of customer dissatisfaction were identified and studied by the team. To determine key problem areas, two customer feedback sources were used in the analysis: a customer survey and feedback from the customer call centre department.

The customer survey included a questionnaire (as shown in Figure CS.1f) and asked customers to rate the level of customer service they received from the ASCs. The questions asked in the survey ranged from how customers were treated on the phone and/or face to face to their perception of the performance of the repair service in form of speed and quality of repair. The survey results rated each survey answer from I (excellent) to IV (poor). Customers were also asked to provide specific comments on how to improve ASC service levels.

Survey results

The customer survey showed clearly that key areas which required improvement were related to repair speed and communications (Figure CS.1g). It was found that customers believed that repair speed might not have been rated as low had the customer been contacted during the repair cycle. Basically, if the customer were updated with the repair status the impact of poor repair turnaround time would have less of an impact. In fact, many customers mentioned that if they knew upfront about a delay they would make other arrangements, such as hiring a replacement product or arranging a loan set from the service centre.

In addition to the customer survey, customer complaints logged in Sony Australia call centre were also tracked and the causes for complaints analysed. The call centre feedback confirmed that some of the commonly occurring complaints were related to ASCs' inability to inform end users on the progress of their repair. In most cases customers had to call the service centre to check on the job status, which annoyed the customers extremely. It was also found that, in some cases, the manner in which the ASC personnel greeted the customer, especially via the telephone, was causing customer dissatisfaction.

Since the survey result showed that current status of customer satisfaction (process mean) was 3.0 (good), it was decided that it would be realistic to improve customer satisfaction to somewhere between the 3.0 and 3.5 range (good/excellent). The improvement target was set as a 3.3 rating by the end of 2002.

From customer surveys and customer communication centre (CCC) feedback, it was confirmed that a problem with customer communications existed in the repair cycle. The basis for improvement therefore was ensuring that the Sony service centre network improved their customer communication to avoid customer service complaints.

The analyse phase identified the factors which had an impact on the project target, and separated those with critical impact from the less important ones. This provided the project team with a clear picture of what improvement actions were required and what their priority was. Figure CS.1h illustrates the use of a CE chart for this purpose.

A failure-mode-and-effect-analysis (FMEA) chart was utilized to identify potential risks associated with those critical items and their possible solutions (improvement actions). Some of these risks and their improvement actions have been included in Figure CS.1i.

In the improve phase a detailed list was prepared consisting of the improvement actions and other relevant activities. A Gantt chart was used to schedule the implementation of these activities into a timeline, as shown in Figure CS.1j.

SONY

REPAIR OPERATION SURVEY QUESTIONNAIRE				
Q.1	Which Sony product did you have serviced?			
	Model No:		Serial No:	
Q.2	Nature of fault?			
Q.3	Who did you initially contact for repair service?			
	❏ i. Sony Call Centre	❏ ii. Dealer	❏ iii. Authorised Sony Service Centre	❏ iv. Independent Service Company
Q.4	Please describe your repair:-			
	❏ i. Carry-in to service centre	❏ ii. In-home Service	❏ iii. Pick-up (by Servicer)	
Q.5	Repair charge?			
	❏ i. In Warranty (FOC)	❏ ii. Chargeable	❏ iii. Out of warranty but covered by Sony (FOC)	
Q.6	Please rate your experience with the repair of your Sony product:-			
	❏ i. Excellent	❏ ii. Good	❏ iii. Fair	❏ iv. Poor
Q.7	Was the unit working properly when you received it back from the service centre?			
	❏ Yes	❏ No		
Q.8	Would you use the Sony Authorised Service Centre again?			
	❏ Yes	❏ No		
Q.9	How would you rate your Sony repair experience on the following issues:-			

		Excellent	*Good*	*Fair*	*Poor*
SERVICE CENTRE					
9a	Location	i. ❏	ii. ❏	iii. ❏	iv. ❏
9b	Opening hours	i. ❏	ii. ❏	iii. ❏	iv. ❏
9c	Appearance	i. ❏	ii. ❏	iii. ❏	iv. ❏
SERVICE PERSONNEL					
9d	Knowledge	i. ❏	ii. ❏	iii. ❏	iv. ❏
9e	Courtesy	i. ❏	ii. ❏	iii. ❏	iv. ❏
9f	Responsiveness	i. ❏	ii. ❏	iii. ❏	iv. ❏
9g	Communications	i. ❏	ii. ❏	iii. ❏	iv. ❏
REPAIR					
9h	Quality	i. ❏	ii. ❏	iii. ❏	iv. ❏
9i	Speed	i. ❏	ii. ❏	iii. ❏	iv. ❏
	If 'Fair' or 'Poor', give reason for delay if known				
	i. ❏ Technical Delay	ii. ❏ Parts delay	iii. ❏ Service Centre Busy	iv. ❏ Unknown	
9j	Appearance/Condition	i. ❏	ii. ❏	iii. ❏	iv. ❏
9k	Price	i. ❏	ii. ❏	iii. ❏	iv. ❏
9l	Explanation	i. ❏	ii. ❏	iii. ❏	iv. ❏
Any additional comments or questions:					

Thank you very much for your time and co-operation

Figure CS.1f   Customer survey questionnaire

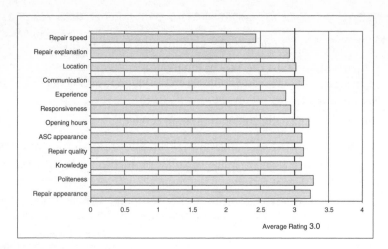

Figure CS.1g   Results of the customer survey 2001

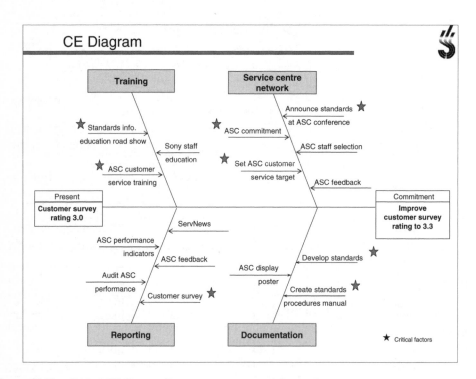

Figure CS.1h   Project CE diagram 'Improve customer satisfaction'

Implementing the Customer Service Standards

A road show was held in each state of Australia, in which Sony management set out the goals for the CS Standards (see Figure CS.1k). Customer survey feedback was cited as examples for the reason to improve. Surprisingly the service centres rallied behind the project and looked forward to participating in the development of the standards.

Risk	Improvement action
Service centre not committing to accept	Perform road show to service centre network and gain their commitment before the project starts
Inappropriate targets set	Work with the service centres to ensure they can accept the standards
Standards fail	Ensure the standards developed deal appropriately with the customer issues identified
Inability to track results	Install a tracking system that measures customer survey feedback
Cost of project too high	Make a budget to cover estimated costs

Figure CS.1i   Risks associated with critical factors and their improvement actions

Task	Sep-01	Oct-01	Nov-01	Dec-01	Jan-02	Feb-02	Mar-02	Apr-02	May-02	Jun-02	Jul-02	Aug-02	Sep-02
									Month due				
ASC Commitment	▓												
Develop standards		▓	▓										
ASC feedback			▓	▓	▓								
Create standards manual			▓	▓	▓	▓							
ASC display material								▓	▓				
Standards release announcement									▓				
Sony staff education			▓	▓									
Standards education road show											▓	▓	
ASC education													
Set ASC customer service target									▓				
Audit ASC performance												▓	▓
Communicate standards via ServNews													▓

Figure CS.1j   Project Gantt chart

The CS Standards were initially drafted by a small team of Sony management and an outside customer service specialist consultant. The draft list of standards were then despatched to all major service centres throughout Australia for comment. Once all the comments were made a final draft of the standards were released for comment at the annual service centre conference in Canberra 2002.

A training manual was written, intended to educate ASCs in each of the 11 standards; it became a reference manual for service centres to use. Once the standards were agreed, the training and reference manual played an important role in the implemetation phase, as it indicated how each standard was to be performed.

An important aspect of the ASCs' acceptance of the standards was their commitment; this was achieved by each ASC and Sony signing the standards poster in front of their peers. This sent a powerful message to Sony that their network of ASCs was willing to adopt the standards.

Once the CS Standards were signed the ASCs were asked to hang the signed standards posters in their reception areas for customers to read (Figure CS.1l).

During 2002 the standards were successfully introduced to the ASC network. In December 2002, a snapshot was taken of customer repairs performed between September and November, which confirmed an increase in customer rating,

Figure CS.1k   Communicating the CS Standards to the ASCs

from 3.0 to 3.1. However, the next major survey, scheduled for the second half of 2003, will provide a much more accurate indicator.

Summary

Six Sigma is all about improving critical processes; it focuses on reducing their variances to improve output. It is a process of making an analysis based on the facts so that a judgement can be made to change/modify the process for the better.

In the case of Sony, customers were complaining when, in their opinion, the process failed or simply when the repair did not go as planned. The objective of Sony's project was to identify where these processes failed and which project to use to rectify this; this would in turn reduce customer dissatisfaction.

After conducting the first Six Sigma project, the team realized that many of the analysis tools that were used by the company were adequate for use within Six Sigma. The Six Sigma methodology was not about inventing new measurement methods; it was, however, about properly analysing the data that had been already collected and stored in the system.

Utilizing the Six Sigma approach, the company determined the critical projects that would make a key difference to improving customer satisfaction. It was also important that these key projects were in line with the corporate targets and goals.

Once the team identified the causes of the variances in the customer repair cycle, they then needed to determine those actions needed for improving the process. The implementation phase was straightforward, due to the thorough analysis of the

SONY Australia Customer Service Standards

1. Our goal is to provide prompt, professional and courteous greeting (phone and face-face) to all customers.

2. To accurately determine customers' needs and answer queries with honesty and integrity.

3. To ensure that all customers details are recorded, confirmed and agreed with the customer.

4. All repairs conducted cost effectively by following Sony repair guidelines by certified staff using genuine spare parts.

5. Our goal is to meet and exceed our mutually agreed completion date.

6. Should any repair alterations or delays be experienced, customers will be promptly contacted.

7. On completion all repair documents will be thoroughly explained and given to customers and any issues will be clarified to ensure satisfaction.

8. This Authorized Service Centre guarantees your repair for 90 days. Should it fail for the same reason, they will promptly take responsibility for this with respect to the original repair.

9. This Authorized Service Centre will provide clean, safe and tidy premises, which also includes the storage and handling of customer's products.

10. Should any of the service conducted not meet the agreed standard, the Authorized Service Centre will follow the Sony agreed complaint and recovery process.

11. Sony will continually monitor the performance of this Authorized Service Centre and feedback will be provided to continually improve the quality of the service provided.

Figure CS.1I   The Sony Australia Customer Service Standards

variances, or areas where the service centres were not performing. The introduction of the CS Standards addressed the key customer concerns of communications. All 11 standards, if followed, would enable the service centre to improve customer satisfaction.

Ongoing surveys to collect customer opinions will ensure that the CS Standards are sustained into the future. The survey results will be used to modify the standards from time to time to ensure that the repair cycle process has the least amount of variances.

Implementing Six Sigma in an Airline Operations Environment

Dr Amin Khan
Malaysia Airlines, Malaysia

Introduction

This paper is an observation and documentary of the way Six Sigma has been introduced in an airline organization and how it has progressed. It does not cover all the facets of the efforts made in its drive towards operational excellence. Instead, it highlights the challenges and the issues the airline faced in making the transition, the success stories that can be drawn, and some lessons that are still emerging in the implementation of Six Sigma in a service organization.

The implementation of Six Sigma started as a productivity initiative in 1995 and evolved in three distinct waves:

• Wave 1 – the productivity drive
• Wave 2 – the transition drive
• Wave 3 – MAS Gemilang[1]

Wave 1 – the productivity drive

Since 1994, the airline had introduced a series of change initiatives in the way it worked and conducted business to respond to changes in the business environment. The intention was to inspire the organization to rebuild itself in ways that respond to the challenges and opportunities in the environment and to meet increasing customer needs. It started with a pilot study of core airline processes. The study was conducted by a group of personnel guided by a consulting firm. Five areas were identified as pilot projects:

• engineering and maintenance
• reservations and ticketing
• passenger services at the airport terminal
• information technology
• corporate planning.

Although the study was successful in identifying potential improvements to enhance revenue and improve costs, and had top management support, the challenge was in implementation, in overcoming the 'not invented here' syndrome.

Wave 2 – the transformation drive

In October 1998, the airline embarked on a change programme, called 'Transformation', to become a customer-focused organization, to broaden its revenue base and to develop a challenged, inspired and team-oriented workforce. Productivity was identified as one of the five strategic initiatives in this change programme. This was not surprising as there was a degree of concern over productivity for the past ten years. Both internal efficiency and utilization efficiency were declining. Most of the macro-level concerns were the result of the concerns at the micro level; for instance, at the check-in counters a problem existed in matching capacity and demand.

A work plan termed 'Productivity by Objectives' was then formulated to identify the target segments in the company operations and prioritize the roll-out. The first phase was to concentrate on the core airline processes with direct customer interface, and the second phase on the supporting management processes.

A simple tool described as MAIC – measure, analyse, improve and control – was introduced to all who were interested and nominated to undertake a productivity improvement 'project'. This was supported by other techniques, such as team dynamics and work group involvement, project management tools, idea generation sessions,

and mentoring. The methodology used is shown in Figure CS.2a.

It was intended that process thinking should firmly be embedded in each and everyone's behaviour and this meant inculcating the culture to all 23 000 employees within the organization. A simple structure, as shown in Figure CS.2b, was thus set up to support this. It comprised the establishment of teams headed by the team leaders in the workplace itself. The team leaders were supported by the departmental management who helped team leaders to introduce and manage change and constructively resolve process conflicts. The teams and their advisors, in turn, were backed up in terms of technical expertise by the Productivity Project Office.

In addition, work was initiated to build the foundation to assure its success:

• training and development plan – to coach project teams using process-based tools, such as process mapping, process

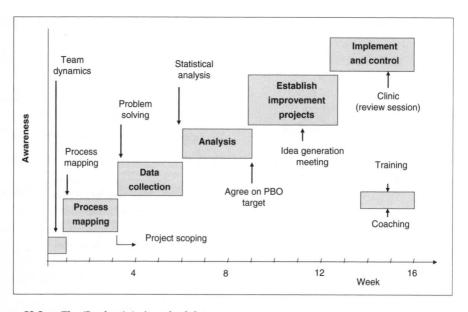

Figure CS.2a   The 'Productivity' methodology

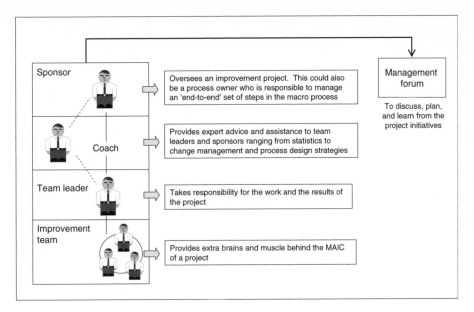

Figure CS.2b   The 'Productivity' reporting structure

and activity based analysis, and statistical process control
- communication plan – to create awareness and generate interest among employees, to provide updates and to disseminate responses to frequently asked questions
- keeping a score mechanism – to track the progress and measure the improvements.

All these activities paved the way for the introduction of Six Sigma in the organization, as shown in Figure CS.2c.

A structured training calendar was published to assist staff in planning their time for training. The training for Six Sigma was initially carried out by Black Belts from General Electric, and this was handed over later to the company's own Black Belts. Management demonstrated its support by its presence and sharing its experience during critical sessions such as during the opening and 'report-out' sessions.

The projects that were undertaken under Wave 2 were at three levels:

- business turnaround level projects (for instance, the catering processes)
- strategic level projects (for instance, in customer handling at the airport terminal)
- problem-solving level projects (for instance, the human resource recruitment process)

Business turnaround level improvement initiatives were driven top-down from the profit and loss line items. In the case of catering, as depicted in Figure CS.2d, the initiatives were tied to the operational budgets and performance. The critical success metrics and actions were thus aligned. The progress in terms of contribution to the bottom line were measured, monitored and manifested on the scoreboards in the Productivity Office in Catering and in the business unit's management report. Quantitative measures, such as cost of production, impact the profit and loss account directly; whereas food and beverage quality and waste are indirect measures.

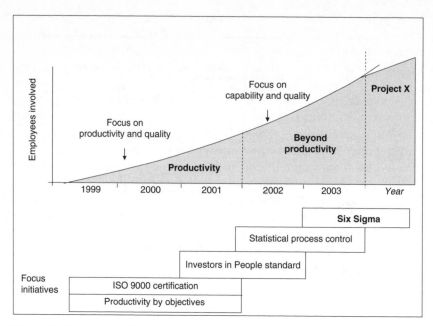

Figure CS.2c   The 'Productivity' blueprint

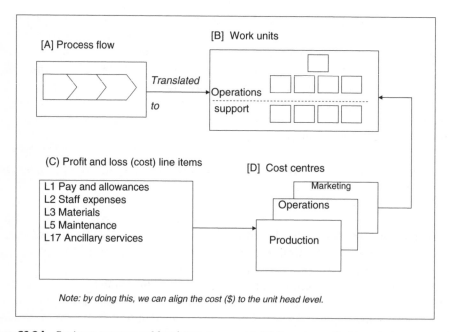

Figure CS.2d   Business turnaround level improvement initiatives as applied to catering

The catering business unit yielded positive results in terms of revenue enhancement and cost improvement, and the first signs of profit about nine months later. Productivity per staff member improved as people became more aware of the measures (Figures CS.2e and CS.2f).

At the strategic and problem-solving levels, however, the success rate was only 50

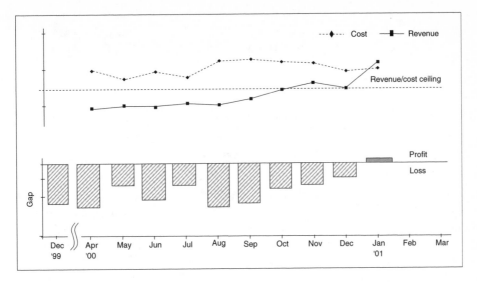

Figure CS.2e   Cost and revenue improvements in catering

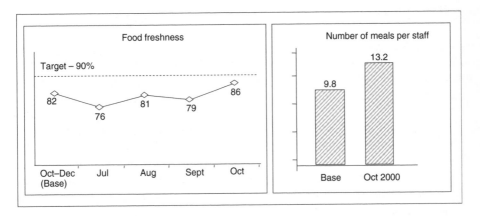

Figure CS.2f   Ratings on freshness and number of meals per staff member

per cent. At a brainstorming session with the team leaders at the management and working levels, the following were identified as possible reasons for the slow progress:

- technical grounds
  - lack of skills
  - lack of critical resources (time, people, and so on)

- political hurdles
  - issues of power and authority
  - threats to the 'old guard'

- discomfort in revealing or showing process deficiencies

- cultural blockades
  - lack of compelling reason (directive, job security, merit or recognition, and so on)
  - old habits and norms
  - peer-group pressure
  - denial syndrome.

As such, it was felt that more leadership visibility was needed to mobilize the

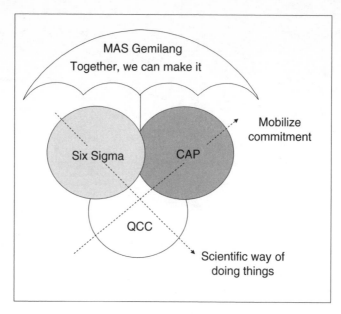

Figure CS.2g   The birth of MAS Gemilang

commitment and energy of the workforce. In this way, MAS Gemilang was born (Figure CS.2g). It was a two-pronged strategy, using:

(a) Six Sigma and QCC (Quality Control Circle) as a technical strategy to build the skills set and
(b) CAP (Change Acceleration Process) as an acceptance strategy to mobilize commitment.

Wave 3 – MAS Gemilang

The vision behind the 'Productivity' journey is best described by the managing director in the preface to the MAS Gemilang launch booklet, which was issued in 2001 (see Figure CS.2h). MAS Gemilang was more than just a combination of the three concepts. It was a fundamental desire of the organization to become an excellent company, the best in its class. In the original words of its chairman, in a speech delivered at the launch on 25 September 2001:

The important thing is to focus, and to align our strategies and energy to that focus. It is our desire to move Malaysia Airlines to a higher platform in the industry. We want to position Malaysia Airlines in the premier league in the industry.

... To focus means we must be clear of our vision and mission. We are operating in the transportation industry as well as in the services industry. From the transportation perspective, our role is basically to transport passengers from one point to another safely, on time, and as comfortably as possible. All the other airlines are basically doing the same thing. What is different is in the service delivery – that personal touch and warmth that we provide to passengers ...

... Our mission then is to provide an airline service to carry passengers from one point to another safely, on time, and

> *Within the next two years, we want to become profitable through changing, adopting, and modifying some of our existing processes and procedures of what and how we do work in the organization. Change can only come about through people. We must be motivated to change; otherwise, change will not occur.*
>
> *MAS Gemilang is the vehicle we have chosen to bring about the desired changes. There are three initiatives that we are putting in place under the umbrella of MAS Gemilang:*
>
> *[1] Change Acceleration Process (CAP) which addresses the human side of acceptance to change.*
>
> *[2] Six Sigma which addresses the technical side of the change process.*
>
> *[3] QCC (Quality Control Circle) to engage everyone in the organization.*
>
> *The Six Sigma methodology is used to facilitate the breakthrough strategy on strategic processes whereas QCC is addressing continuous improvement at the work place.*
>
> *Both Sigma and QCC are meant to improve our work processes towards Six Sigma quality, which literally means zero defect.*
>
> *I am looking forward to your full support on our MAS Gemilang program as it is part of our strategic initiatives to turnaround Malaysia Airlines.*
>
> **Together, we can make it.**

Figure CS.2h   Extract from the MAS Gemilang launch document *MAS Gemilang – Together, We Can Make It* (2001), page 1

comfortably – with that distinct Malaysian personal touch and warmth. Given the mission, we must rally our resources and energy, and align all other activities to achieve that mission. It is do-able, and it must be part of our service culture in the organization.

MAS Gemilang is the vehicle we have chosen to achieve that mission. The goal is viable customer satisfaction through superb service delivery. We do not want a service delivery system that moves passengers in one direction and their bagggage in another.

MAS Gemilang means shining in glory, building success upon success. But it depends on you and me – our commitment and knowledge to move forward. Commitment and knowledge are critical to the success of MAS Gemilang and the achievement of our mission ...

As described by the chairman, the twin banner for MAS Gemilang is 'knowledge' and 'commitment'. The mission of MAS Gemilang is:

To *quantifiably* improve the health of the organization by enhancing the value of services to customers whilst increasing profits.

The word 'quantifiably' embodies the plan to transform the organization into a data-driven organization. Six Sigma was chosen because of its comprehensive quality philosophy about operational excellence that focuses on the customer. It is also a proven, data-driven methodology for improving processes. In using Six Sigma, we inculcate process thinking, base our decisions on data, and understand the variations.

In short, Six Sigma will:

- help the airline fix the process, not the problem
- improve processes even as they don't fail
- provide everyone with a process-based knowledge – to find out root causes and anticipate issues
- impart knowledge to employees and show them how to learn (develop an enquiring mind).

The reason behind QCC was to get everyone involved in the company. Whilst Six Sigma is a top-down approach and mainly targets the management levels and above, the QCC tools are promoted amongst the non-executive, supporting staff.

Whilst Six Sigma and QCC tools were deployed to improve processes, it was crucial that the improvements were sustained and the drive to learn and improve is expanded to the rest of the company. The Change Acceleration Process (CAP) was adopted to complement Six Sigma and QCC.

CAP is a tool to mobilize commitment and manage the transition from the current to a desired state. It helps teams prepare for and conduct planning discussions, encourage continued involvement, and empowers members to improve work performance. It builds teamwork and is a reinforcing theme. Everyone wants to be a winner and part of the winning team, and in the process, more and more people will be drawn in to learn and participate in improving work processes.

As highlighted in the speech of its chairman, Malaysia Airlines selected MAS Gemilang as a vehicle to achieve its mission. The alignment of MAS Gemilang with the company's imperatives is illustrated in Figure CS.2i.

The success of MAS Gemilang hinged to a large extent on the communication plan. A series of road shows and briefings were conducted with the senior management, heads of departments as well as union representatives. In addition, practitioners from General Electric were invited to share their vision and experience. The purpose was to build awareness, energize and reinforce commitment.

Surveys were carried out to objectively gauge the mood and acceptance of the MAS Gemilang programme. The feedback was used in planning – to refine and re-define the training, the communication and the roll-out plan.

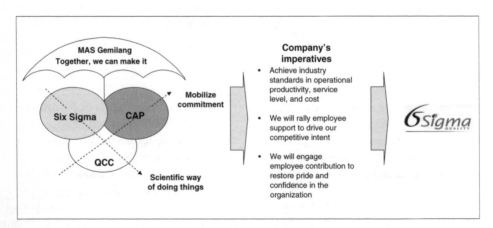

Figure CS.2i   Alignment of MAS Gemilang with company imperatives

Prior to the MAS Gemilang official launch in September 2001, a survey was carried out among 387 employees from all levels in the company. The results showed that whilst there was agreement with the programme, the degree of willingness and commitment diminished with the level of effort required to engage in the training and the employment of the tools (Figure CS.2j).

Similar surveys were carried out during the road shows to assess the factors that could impede the acceptance and progress of MAS Gemilang and identify the risk areas (Figure CS.2k). the following were observed from the survey:

• the most significant factor in preventing MAS Gemilang from moving forward was found to be the attitude amongst the executive and non-executive staff. Staff attitude required further analysis as it was perceived as a complex issue (Figure CS.2l)

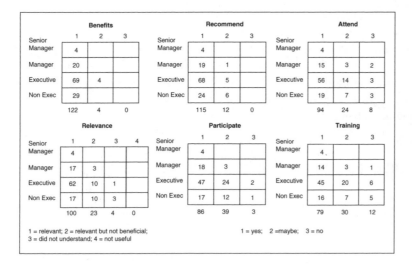

Benefits

	1	2	3
Senior Manager	4		
Manager	20		
Executive	69	4	
Non Exec	29		
	122	4	0

Recommend

	1	2	3
Senior Manager	4		
Manager	19	1	
Executive	68	5	
Non Exec	24	6	
	115	12	0

Attend

	1	2	3
Senior Manager	4		
Manager	15	3	2
Executive	56	14	3
Non Exec	19	7	3
	94	24	8

Relevance

	1	2	3	4
Senior Manager	4			
Manager	17	3		
Executive	62	10	1	
Non Exec	17	10	3	
	100	23	4	0

Participate

	1	2	3
Senior Manager	4		
Manager	18	3	
Executive	47	24	2
Non Exec	17	12	1
	86	39	3

Training

	1	2	3
Senior Manager	4		
Manager	14	3	1
Executive	45	20	6
Non Exec	16	7	5
	79	30	12

1 = relevant; 2 = relevant but not beneficial;
3 = did not understand; 4 = not useful

1 = yes;   2 =maybe;   3 = no

Figure CS.2j   Results of a survey carried out during the MAS awareness briefing

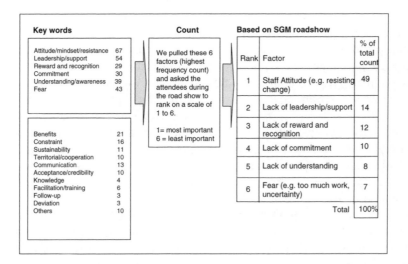

Key words

Attitude/mindset/resistance	67
Leadership/support	54
Reward and recognition	29
Commitment	30
Understanding/awareness	39
Fear	43

Benefits	21
Constraint	16
Sustainability	11
Territorial/cooperation	10
Communication	13
Acceptance/credibility	10
Knowledge	4
Facilitation/training	6
Follow-up	3
Deviation	3
Others	10

Count

We pulled these 6 factors (highest frequency count) and asked the attendees during the road show to rank on a scale of 1 to 6.

1= most important
6 = least important

Based on SGM roadshow

Rank	Factor	% of total count
1	Staff Attitude (e.g. resisting change)	49
2	Lack of leadership/support	14
3	Lack of reward and recognition	12
4	Lack of commitment	10
5	Lack of understanding	8
6	Fear (e.g. too much work, uncertainty)	7
	Total	100%

Figure CS.2k   Factors that could prevent MAS Gemilang moving forward

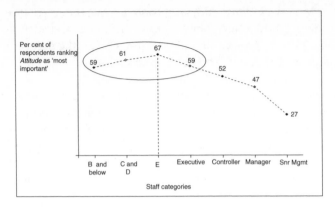

Figure CS.2I Analysis of survey responses to keyword 'attitude'

- lack of leadership and support and lack of reward and recognition were ranked as the next highest factors. These were perceived as management issues
- lack of understanding and fear were perceived as issues arising from lack of knowledge and could be addressed through greater and better communication as well as training and coaching.

In addition, the survey results provided valuable information on acceptance of the tools:

- Six Sigma and QCC appeared to be widely accepted
- QCC seemed to be more acceptable amongst the non-executive staff in Grade E and below
- those with more than 15 years of service as well as managers and above were not keen to sign up for training.

The survey also gauged the level of acceptance by division. The IT division and technical and ground operations (TGO) in Kuala Lumpur International Airport showed the lowest level of acceptance to Six Sigma. Both these divisions are core to the airline operations. As such, these two areas were assessed to be the greatest challenge in terms of gaining acceptance.

The major issues identified and action plans to address them included:

- senior general managers must reinforce the importance of knowledge and the use of the MAS Gemilang tools pertinent to their work unit's individual business and operating environment and to champion success stories
- senior general managers must stimulate and motivate those managers with more than 21 years of service to embrace the tools in MAS Gemilang
- more focus group discussions must be used to break through the attitude challenge confronting the progress of MAS Gemilang.

Based on the survey findings, a communications strategy was formulated (shown in Figure CS.2m). The MAS Gemilang programme was officially launched on 25 September 2001 by the chairman of the company. By then, it was possible to showcase how MAS Gemilang had evolved and was embraced by the organization.

A snapshot was taken on the health of the MAS Gemilang programme six months after the launch. A total of about 300 staff were trained, and the number of projects

	30 July	6 Aug	13 Aug	20 Aug	27 Aug	3 Sept
Briefing the senior general managers	▓	▓				
Awareness campaign to heads of department		▓	▓	▓		
Senior general manager's road show		▓	▓	▓	▓	
Contact with union representatives		▓	▓			
Presentation by General Electric		▓	▓			
Managing Director's message		▓	▓			▓
Sharing success stories	▓	▓	▓	▓	▓	
Launch of MAS Gemilang	▓					▓

Figure CS.2m   MAS Gemilang implementation plan

had mushroomed to 119 projects. These yielded an estimated savings of RM 10.1 million and revenue protection of RM 90 million, as shown in Figure CS.2n.

The spread of the number of initiated projects and staff trained among the divisions is shown in Figure CS.2o. The TGO division had initiated the most number of projects and the largest number of staff trained although the earlier survey showed a relatively lower level of acceptance.

It was observed that, since the start of MAS Gemilang, it was taking greater effort to kick off and complete projects. In a typical batch of Six Sigma participants, it was noted that as the training and project progressed, the retention was diminishing (Figure CS.2p). This phenomenon supported the earlier survey finding that the level of commitment decreased as the level of effort and involvement required increased.

Thus, CAP became a very important tool in building commitment and re-energizing the team in process improvement.

A year after MAS Gemilang was launched, a convention was held to share the learnings and to reward the effort and energy staff had put into the programme. It provided a platform for the company to spotlight the success stories. In conjunction with the convention, staff who made outstanding contributions in using Six

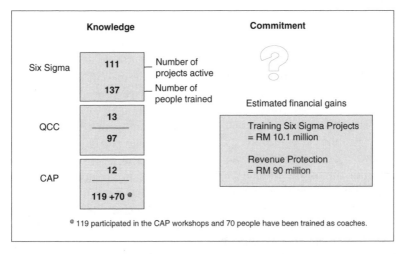

Figure CS.2n   Snapshot taken six months after the launch of MAS Gemilang

No. of projects	TGO	Cargo	Flight Ops	Sales	Network	IT	Finance	Corp. services	Audit	Total
Six Sigma	45	15	12	7	0	3	18	10	1	111
QCC	8	1	0	2	0	1	1	0	0	13
CAP	4	1	1	4	0	0	1	1	0	12
Total	**57**	**17**	**13**	**13**	**0**	**4**	**20**	**11**	**1**	**136**

No. of staff trained	TGO	Cargo	Flight Ops	Sales	Network	IT	Finance	Corp. services	Audit	Total
Six Sigma	61	17	12	11	1	4	19	11	1	137
QCC	45	8	4	11	1	9	6	12	1	97
CAP	56	18	15	39	5	5	21	25	5	189
Total	**162**	**43**	**31**	**61**	**7**	**18**	**46**	**48**	**7**	**423**

Figure CS.2o   Breakdown of the number of initiated projects and staff trained in divisions

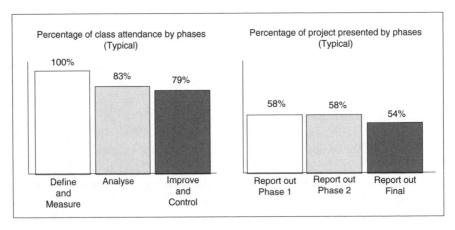

Figure CS.2p   Level of commitment shown as the percentage of participation in Six Sigma training and project reporting

Sigma, QCC and CAP tools were recognized as champions. The reason for having the convention culminate with the awards was to reinforce the message for the company to be process- and data-driven; it was also to motivate and to rally further the commitment. The awards were designed to add impetus to the programme. The convention saw a gathering of Six Sigma practitioners from the airline industry and other service and manufacturing industries. It reaffirmed the need to press on for consistency in excellence and to drive the company's decision-making and processes based on knowledge.

Early results

In the cargo area, where the survey revealed a high risk of staff attitude challenges, the CAP project proved extremely successful. One of the CAP projects was to reduce the incidents of incorrect offloading of cargo by 15 per cent and 25 per cent within three months. The results exceeded expectations in both stepped targets. Another significant improvement result was achieved by the TGO division in 'Short shipping of customers' baggage' (Figure CS.2q).

In the front office, Six Sigma resulted in

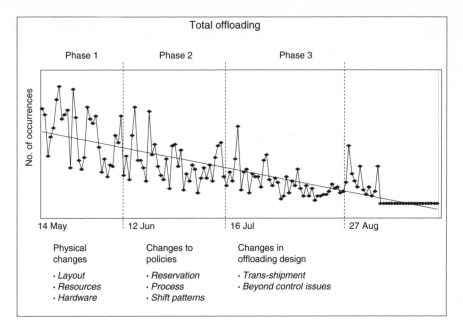

Figure CS.2q   Improvements in 'Short shipping of customers' baggage'

remarkable improvements in 'Call centre productivity' as shown in Figure CS.2r.

Summary

The MAS Gemilang projects yielded quantifiable results that were firmly tied to the company's imperatives. The journey continues with the human resource directive for all executives to undertake a process improvement project. In the network division, the managers in charge are now all Six Sigma tools for their route

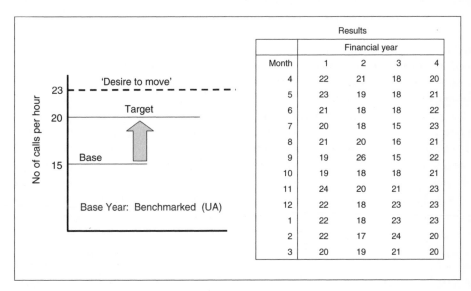

Figure CS.2r   'Call centre productivity' improvements

analysis and network planning. It was a division that had initially resisted the tools, as seen from the preliminary survey; but it is now one of the best equipped and most data-driven. In information technology, which was a high risk potential area, the MAS Gemilang programme has been re-launched in the entire division recently.

It should be remembered that the MAS Gemilang projects were primarily based on the individual participants choosing to join and learn the tools. The projects are not yet driven by the business metrics. A more structured approach would be to drive it from the business metrics, as in the case of the catering business unit; support it with training and mentoring and linking the initiatives to the performance appraisal system. Though it is still only a simmering fire, given the robustness of the programme, it will be congruent to its name – shining from glory to glory – as the tools are put to use from crafting strategy to coaching operations.

Notes

1. MAS Gemilang: 'MAS' stands for Malaysia Airlines System; 'Gemilang' is a Malay word which can be translated into English as 'shining in glory'. In 2001, Malaysia Airlines named its business improvement programme 'MAS Gemilang'.

Building an Effective Internal Customer Service Focus and Relationship

Ms Vanessa Craig
Queensland Rail, Australia

Introduction

This case study traces the path that Queensland Rail (QR) Workshops travelled in its productivity improvement journey. The journey did not begin without there being first a thinking through and stepping out of the actions that led to the selection of Six Sigma as the most appropriate methodology for QR Workshops to enable them to deliver cost-effective and operationally excellent support services to the QR business groups that service QR's customers. Workshops Group is defined as a support group in QR's structure as it does not service QR's customers directly; rather it provides rolling stock maintenance and overhaul to QR's coal and freight group and passenger group. It is defined as an internal service provider with its primary aim being to enable its customers to provide the most cost-effective and seamless service to their customers: QR's travelling public, the coal industry and agriculture.

The implementation of Six Sigma in QR Workshops is in its early stages; therefore the major focus of the case study is on the preparation of the foundation and the introduction of Six Sigma.

The implementation environment: QR the organization

QR is a diverse and interesting business. It is a vertically integrated and commercially focused transport and logistics corporation operating Australia's largest integrated rail network. Annual operating revenue is in excess of \$2 billion. It owns assets worth \$7 billion and employs a workforce of approximately 13 700.

Comprising the three sites in Rockhampton, Redbank and Townsville, QR's major activities include (Figure CS.3a):

- the provision of heavy haul transport services to the state's mining, minerals processing and electricity generation industries
- the transportation of container traffic and bulk fuels between major industrial, regional and mining centres
- the movement of livestock, sugar, grain and other primary produce between centres
- door-to-door services for general freight with links to Sydney and Melbourne

Figure CS.3a   Map of Queensland Rail network and Workshops locations

- the supply of safe, fast and comfortable commuter passenger rail travel in South East Queensland
- the provision of tourist and long-distance rail passenger services and
- the provision of rail technology and expertise to the railway industry worldwide: QR provides consultancy in 32 countries.

The QR organizational management structure

QR is divided into several business groups under the control of a group general manager (GGM). In each group is a series of divisions, each under the control of a general manager (GM).

The key attributes of QR's organizational design framework include:

- an external customer focus primarily through the coal and freight services, and passenger services business groups
- the Network Access Group who manage the interface with all users of the rail infrastructure, allocating track slots and managing the scheduling and control of trains, the access of trains to the track and maintenance of the track
- a structure of support groups that provide internal support services at efficient cost. These include:
  - the Infrastructure Services Group who build and maintain track, signalling, station buildings, hard stands, depots
  - the Workshops Group who overhaul and repair locomotives and rolling stock

- the Technical Services Group who design rolling stock, signalling systems, telecommunications, electrical and train operational systems
- the Corporate Services Group who provide management systems for supply (strategic sourcing, inventory management), human resource services, legal services and fleet management
- the Finance Group, who provide financial services
- the Strategy Unit, who provide strategic planning, marketing, and business improvement direction, frameworks, and processes.

The winds of change

QR is historically rich, as it has been in operation for over 130 years, and the Workshops function has been part of this operation from the earliest days. From its establishment in the 1870s the Queensland Government Railways (as QR was then known) enjoyed relative stability and growth. It was a significant government tool for building the prosperity potential of the state, as the railway was used to open up Queensland to settlement and agriculture. The emphasis was on service, coverage of the state and full employment. During that time the railway was a major employer in the state, and was subject to tight government control, including a close control of all investment decisions and even direct intervention in labour practices, such as ordering the reversal of merit selection for staff back to seniority. Even as late as 1970 women were required to resign their employment upon marriage.

The year 1991 heralded a time of significant change for the Queensland Rail organization. With 25 000 staff, QR underwent a major restructure and

commenced a significant reform programme designed to bring about customer focus, increased productivity and a more commercial operation. These changes were initiated by the state government as part of the move to prepare Australia for open competition. Award restructuring was initiated to reposition the organization's labour force. By 2002 staff numbers had been reduced to 13 700, a reduction of almost 50 per cent. During the same time the Workshops staff were reduced from 2393 to 1580, a reduction of 40 per cent.

Between 1991 and 2000 QR underwent several restructures and numerous improvement initiatives:

- award restructuring
- quality assurance
- total quality management
- the Australian Quality Award Framework.

QR Workshops embraced quality assurance and also embarked on a significant business restructuring and turnaround programme called the 'Workshops Redevelopment Programme'. This programme involved major expenditure in new facilities and new equipment in the three workshop sites of Redbank, Rockhampton and Townsville. A significant improvement in productivity was achieved during this time, but the culture of the workforce remained relatively unchanged, because repositioning of the leadership and workforce skill set did not take place.

Looking for results: Workshops' main reasons for implementing Six Sigma

One of the tenets of the Workshops Redevelopment Programme between 1995 and 2000 was to bring in new business based on the forecast reduction of business from

QR – which had always in the past been the major customer. An unfortunate and unintended consequence of this was that Workshops lost some of their focus on their most important customer and some Workshops business decisions had major adverse impacts on QR's customers.

In 1999 another QR restructure resulted in the appointment of a new GGM to Workshops with a mandate to turn around the by then tenuous customer relationship with the QR Business Group customers, and simultaneously to increase productivity and involve the Workshops staff in those improvements. In 2000 the Workshops GGM initiated a significant refocusing programme to achieve the required turnaround.

This refocusing was designed by a partnership between Workshops quality environment and safety manager and the QR corporate business improvement manager, and was called the 'Business Improvement Programme'. It had a triple focus:

a.   Improving customer satisfaction
b.   Developing leadership capability
c.   Improving staff satisfaction.

The first step was to identify the start point in order to design improvement strategies customized to Workshops culture.

Improving customer satisfaction

CAPTURING THE VOICE OF THE CUSTOMER

A customer survey process was designed to measure the current level of customer satisfaction, and, in its implementation, both to identify sufficiently detailed information on problems so that they could effectively be resolved, and to commence rebuilding the relationship between Workshops and its customers. The process was thus both customer satisfaction measurement and the first stage of customer relationship management.

The following categories of satisfaction were measured in 2000:

1.   Timeliness
2.   Consultation
3.   Quality
4.   Innovation
5.   Communication
6.   Value for money.

These categories were designed to be aggregated to the QR Corporate Balanced Scorecard 'Dashboard' (Figure CS.3b).

The customer survey process consisted of the following steps:

- all Workshops customers were identified, as were their management representatives (65 in all, as many customers identified others who could inform the nature of the problems that the customers experienced)
- a one-hour structured interview was held with each customer representative, by teams of two or three representatives from Corporate Business Improvement, as customers refused to talk openly direct to Workshops management whom they viewed at that time as the wilful cause of the problem (see Figure CS.3c)
- all the identified problems were recorded, by product and service type, exactly as the teams were told in order to retain the true essence of the problems
- quantitative data were analysed and incorporated in a presentation for feedback to Workshops management
- the qualitative comment information about the problems was examined,

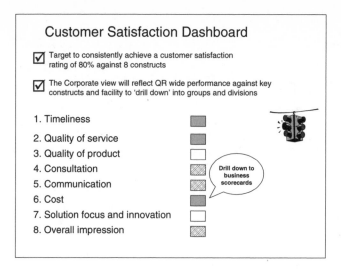

Figure CS.3b   QR Corporate Customer Satisfaction Dashboard

summarized and grouped under product and service, as a foundation for recommending appropriate actions
- appropriate actions to address the problems were identified and captured in recommendations to be implemented during the following year
- results – both summarized qualitative data and quantitative data – were presented to the Workshops management team as one of the inputs in the yearly planning session
- written, widely distributed feedback was provided to the customers on the common themes among the problems they had identified: to publicly recognize the tough message Workshops had been given and to make a public commitment to customers on exactly what Workshops were going to do to address the problems. This letter was sent to all customers who were interviewed. It was an unusually brave act on the part of Workshops management considering the size of the problem that had been identified. The presentation given to Workshops management in the planning was made available to anyone who asked to see it.

Results of the 2000 customer survey

An improvement priorities map, as shown in Figure CS.3d, was used to classify and prioritize areas for improvement from the customer survey results. The lowest ratings were (on a seven-point scale where 1 = lowest and 7 = highest):

- innovation (3.18)
- value for money (3.19)
- timeliness (3.21)
- communication (3.46).

However, the gap between satisfaction and importance assisted in identifying the critical challenges, as shown in Figure CS.3e, as follows:

1. Timeliness
2. Value for money
3. Quality (of service rather than product, as many customers differentiated this in their comments)
4. Communication.

The relationship was stormy: some illustrative comments from the first Workshops customer survey were:

Please circle the most appropriate rating		
	Performance	Importance
	1 = Very poor 4 = Satisfactory 7 = Very well	1 = Of no importance 4 = Medium importance 7 = Very important
How well has Workshops Group...?		
1. Delivered products/services by the agreed time	1 2 3 4 5 6 7	1 2 3 4 5 6 7
2. Consulted to assess your needs	1 2 3 4 5 6 7	1 2 3 4 5 6 7
3. Delivered products at the right quality	1 2 3 4 5 6 7	1 2 3 4 5 6 7
4. Delivered services at the right quality	1 2 3 4 5 6 7	1 2 3 4 5 6 7
5. Shown innovation in meeting your needs	1 2 3 4 5 6 7	1 2 3 4 5 6 7
6. Effectively communicated work progress	1 2 3 4 5 6 7	1 2 3 4 5 6 7
7. Provided you with value for money	1 2 3 4 5 6 7	1 2 3 4 5 6 7
	Performance	
	1 = Significantly declined 4 = Stayed the same 7 = Significantly improved	
Compared to last time, how would you rank Workshops Group's Performance?		
8. Delivered products/services by the agreed time	1 2 3 4 5 6 7	
9. Consulted to assess your needs	1 2 3 4 5 6 7	
10. Delivered products at the right quality	1 2 3 4 5 6 7	
11. Delivered services at the right quality	1 2 3 4 5 6 7	
12. Shown innovation in meeting your needs	1 2 3 4 5 6 7	
13. Effectively communicated work progress	1 2 3 4 5 6 7	
14. Provided you with value for money	1 2 3 4 5 6 7	

15. Overall, how satisfied were you with the products/services provided by Workshops Group?

1	2	3	4	5	6	7
Very dissatisfied			Just OK			Very satisfied

16. Please rate how easy is it to do business with Workshops Group

1	2	3	4	5	6	7
Very difficult			Just OK			Very easy

17. How could Workshops make it easier for you to do business with them?
18. Are there any particular product/services that you consider need improvement?
19. Please rate Workshops understanding of your business

1	2	3	4	5	6	7
No understanding			Fair understanding			High understanding

20. In what ways is the working relationship between Workshops Group and your area working well?
21. In what ways can the working relationship between Workshops Group and your area be improved?
22. What are the major challenges facing your business in the future?

23. Any general comments? _____
_____
_____

Figure CS.3c   Customer survey questionnaire

'Workshops break my heart.'
'Terrible to deal with.'
'WS culture of aggressive and antagonistic "bull in a china shop".'
'Spend most time trying to score points off customers, makes you want to have nothing to do with them.'

Over the next 18 months emphasis was placed on improving the relationship with customers by improving the above four critical challenges. However, in terms of improving timeliness and quality Workshops did not have a methodology to systematically tackle the problems in a way

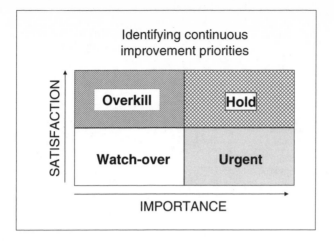

Figure CS.3d   Improvement priorities map used to interpret customer survey results

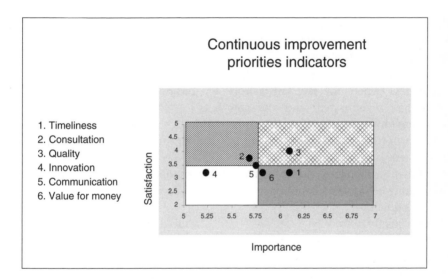

Figure CS.3e   2000 customer survey results

that would deliver robust and significant improvement outcomes. The significance of this was to be revealed in the second customer survey, run in late 2002.

Results of the 2002 customer survey

By the time the second survey was run, in late 2002, the relationship Workshops had with its customers had improved significantly; so much so, that the structured one-hour interviews were administered by a team of Workshops own quality, environment and safety (QES) unit staff, guided and supplemented by Corporate Business Improvement. There were no refusals to any of the 68 interviews requested. Workshops QES staff recorded and analysed the data and, under guidance from the QR corporate business improvement manager, developed the recommendations to be presented to the Workshops management team's strategic planning session in November 2002.

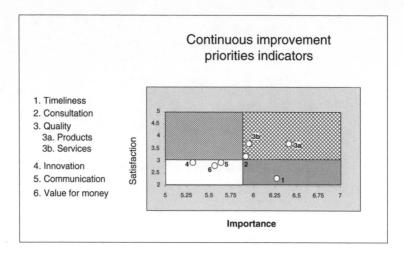

Figure CS.3f　2002 customer survey results

Critical imperatives identified in the 2002 customer survey, as shown in Figure CS.3f were, in order of priority:

1. Timeliness (where the raw satisfaction score had deteriorated, and the gap between importance and performance had grown wider during the intervening two years)
2. Consultation (agreeing exactly what is to be done before work commences)
3. Product quality
4. Service quality.

Although satisfaction scores had improved on some criteria, the gap between satisfaction and importance had widened. This was because the pressure on the QR customers was increasing at a greater rate than Workshops' rate of improvement. The comments from the 2002 survey were full of compliments for, and reinforcement of, the partnership approach Workshops had embarked upon.

Comments from the second Workshops survey

Q21. In what ways is the working relationship between Workshops Group and your area working well?

'Things have definitely gotten better since last time (global perception).'
'Networking is working well.'
'Communications between the businesses has improved.'

Although value for money had improved significantly, the message in the qualitative data was that if there were two things Workshops could do for their customers, they were:

1. Speed up the timeliness of delivery of rolling stock back into service
2. Drive down the costs of rolling stock repair.

Q17. How could Workshops make it easier for you to do business with them?

'From past experience with Workshops, we have to order early and build extra time into our business project plans to anticipate Workshops' delays and shortfalls.'
'On-time delivery of components – we can't sweat the assets if we don't have the components to keep them on the track.'

'Break down barriers to get the supply chain to work.'
'Try harder to be more commercially focused and competitive with outside industry.'

Clearly, an improvement methodology was called for that would create a significantly greater rate of improvement than had been used in the past.

An examination of the QR cost structure in 2000 had identified that 50 per cent of the costs were located in the supply chain, both internal and external. This finding commenced a major supply chain initiative to implement strategic sourcing.

Taking the temperature of the workforce (staff surveys)

Parallel to the customer surveys, QR also conducted staff surveys. 2000 staff survey findings across QR revealed that staff experienced significant frustration with all aspects of the supply chain. Exploration of the low ratings revealed the cause as internal coordination and hand-offs ('hand-offs' are when work moves along the flow between organizational units within Workshops itself, creating delays) between organizational units as well as the procurement of goods and services from inside and outside QR.

This is illustrated in the patterns of high and low ratings in the staff survey: both items (single questions) and constructs (groups of items). See Figures CS.3g and CS.3h.

A strong commitment to continuous improvement, to integration across boundaries and to customer service is evident, coupled with frustration at the lack of a robust, participative mechanism to make the required improvements to service levels.

Workshops Group itself was faced with a steadily increasing shortfall in its target of break-even financial contribution to the wider organization. This was caused by Workshops absorbing the cost overruns on projects that were incurred by poor planning, programming and organizing of work. The work required tight coordination across numerous organizational boundaries for it to flow smoothly, without delays. This was not happening, and much of the cause was outside Workshops' control.

Learning from previous change

Item	Mean	Sd	N	Item description
High Scoring Items				(Strengths)
Q13	3.45	.60	3198	Continuous improvement necessary for future of QR
Q52	3.44	.63	3202	I take pride in the way I do my work
Q14	3.25	.62	3200	Staff in other div./sections treated with due respect
Q53	3.04	.69	3198	Work team gives customers excellent quality service
Q58	3.03	.82	3201	'One QR' can become a reality if we all work together
Low Scoring Items				(Opportunities)
Q42*	1.90	.76	3185	Internal suppliers need to improve quality/services
Q26*	1.91	.78	3166	External suppliers need to improve quality/services
Q51*	1.91	.67	3181	Need upgraded service capability for quality service
Q20*	1.93	.78	3181	Decision making concentrated within a small group
Q21*	1.95	.68	3194	Better measures of activities needed to provide service
Response scores: Maximum = 4 (Strongly agree) Minimum = 1 (Strongly disagree)				

Figure CS.3g   2000 QR staff survey results: five highest and lowest scoring items

Rank	Construct	Mean	Sd	+/ -	N	Description
1	C2	2.92	.52	+	3123	Processes
2	C1	2.83	.47	+	3114	Customers
3	C8	2.65	.57	+	3090	Performance
4	C4	2.60	.60	+	3088	Measurement
5	C5	2.55	.59	+	3099	People
6	C10	2.49	.70	–	3151	Culture
7	C7	2.49	.71	–	3062	Leadership
8	C6	2.36	.61	–	3122	Planning
9	C9	2.32	.60	–	3095	Communication
10	C3	2.19	.47	–	3125	Suppliers

(Note: Scale 1 = very poor, 2 = poor, 3 = good, 4 = excellent)

Tinted fields are used to illustrate priority areas for improvement:
Grey shaded fields = score below 2.5 therefore highest priority for improvement
Striped fields = score between 2.5 (which is the half way point) and 2.75 therefore
second priority for improvement
White field = score above 2.75 therefore not a priority for improvement at this time

Figure CS.3h 2000 QR staff survey results: constructs statistics

initiatives driven by QR Corporate Business Improvement, it was clear that interactive and empowerment oriented quality improvement initiatives that had worked very well in other parts of QR were not well received in the Workshops culture. A much more structured quality improvement/process improvement methodology would be required.

For the many reasons above Six Sigma was selected as the only methodology that would suit the Workshops culture and deliver the depth and extent of improvements required of Workshops Group in the short time frame available for such a significant turnaround for QR.

Developing leadership capability

Many comments from the customer survey had identified Workshops leadership capability as a significant part of the problem, particularly the management of staff and management of projects. Profiling of leadership roles was undertaken as a

foundation for building managerial leadership capability. This would provide the leadership behaviours required to drive the desired Workshops culture and commercial managerial skills. They were designed to provide the basis for leader selection, performance management and skills development and succession management programmes. In particular a focus was created on:

- leading with vision and values
- customer focus
- building partnerships
- building trust
- commercial acumen.

Improving staff satisfaction

In 2000 Workshops had run the comprehensive staff satisfaction survey designed around the Australian Business Excellence Framework. This survey was run again in 2002. The 2000 survey results, along with the customer survey, provided the baseline against which to measure the effectiveness of the Workshops Business

Improvement Programme. The survey contained 58 questions rated on a four-point scale where 4 was high and 1 was low. The questions were grouped into ten constructs against which Workshops could track the improvements of both its people initiatives and its progress in improving its business management processes as defined by the Australian Business Excellence Framework. Results for 2000 are shown in Figure CS.3i.

It was possible to identify specific items within constructs that required improvement. An analysis of the 2000 staff survey results revealed that almost all items across all constructs that involved performance measures or performance indicators, process capability or a shared process improvement methodology, rated low (Figure CS.3j).

Although most constructs, and items within them (particularly 'Customers' and 'Culture' – the latter measuring shared understanding of strategic direction) had improved by the time the second survey was run in 2002, the specific selection of items above had not improved at all.

The decision was made after analysing the 2002 results (Figure CS.3k) that what was required was a shared process improvement methodology that would

Item	Mean	SD	N	Item description
High scoring items				**(Strengths)**
Q13	3.43	.60	1388	Continuous improvement necessary for future of QR
Q52	3.40	.70	1387	I take pride in the way I do my work
Q14	3.19	.62	1390	Staff in other divisions/sections treated with respect
Q53	3.01	.72	1386	Work team provides excellent quality customer service
Q58	2.93	.87	1387	'ONE QR' can become a reality if all work together
Low scoring items				**(Opportunities)**
Q20*	1.80	.76	1380	Decision making concentrated within a small group
Q26*	1.88	.78	1375	External suppliers need to improve quality of G & S
Q31*	1.91	.90	1385	Senior managers behaviour not consistent with words
Q23*	1.93	.88	1390	Poor verbal communication sometimes causes problems
Q51*	1.93	.70	1382	Need to upgrade service capability for quality service

KEY
Scores: Maximum = 4 (strongly agree) Minimum = 1 (strongly disagree)

Figure CS.3i   2000 Workshops staff survey; five highest and lowest scoring items

Rank	Construct	Mean	SD	+/–	N	Description
1	C2	2.86	.53	+	1344	Processes
2	C1	2.74	.51	+	1340	Customers
3	C8	2.52	.59	+	1322	Performance
4	C4	2.50	.63	+	1338	Measurement
5	C5	2.38	.60	–	1332	People
6	C10	2.34	.67	–	1354	Culture
7	C7	2.30	.71	–	1329	Leadership
8	C6	2.28	.61	–	1344	Planning
9	C9	2.20	.59	–	1336	Communication
10	C3	2.19	.48	–	1359	Suppliers

Figure CS.3j   2000 Workshops staff survey results: constructs statistics

Rank	Construct	Mean	SD	+/-	N	Description
1	C2	2.89	.50	+	824	Processes
2	C1	2.88	.41	+	805	Customers
3	C8	2.58	.56	+	797	Performance
4	C10	2.56	.65	+	817	Culture
5	C4	2.52	.61	+	803	Measurement
6	C5	2.42	.58	-	811	People
7	C6	2.32	.61	-	814	Planning
8	C7	2.31	.70	-	805	Leadership
9	C9	2.20	.58	-	810	Communication
10	C3	2.14	.45	-	821	Suppliers

Figure CS.3k   2002 Workshops staff survey results: constructs statistics

deliver a robust suite of in-process measures, and process outcome measures and that would enable effective management and improvement of process capability.

Although processes and customers rated the highest of the constructs, the message from the customers was that, from their perspective, neither meeting their needs as customers nor management of processes to deliver the outcomes they required, was good.

Interestingly, managers from customer parts of QR said they found the Workshops staff very customer-focused and their individual work quality good.

LISREL is linear structural relationship mapping, a powerful and rigorous statistical analysis technique that can be applied to large-scale survey results, which plots the relationships between the constructs of a survey – in this case the constructs of the staff satisfaction survey. Arrows are drawn to illustrate which constructs have a relationshp with which other constructs, with numbers on them to identify the strength of the relationship. The flow of relationships in a causative manner goes from left to right, across the sets of boxes. A LISREL analysis (causative mapping) of the staff survey results revealed staff perceived poor leadership to be their major

impediment in improving service to the customer (Figure CS.3l).

Again, Six Sigma was reinforced as an appropriate methodology to meet the need, as it focuses on the customer and drives operational excellence through the organization's leadership.

External pressures on QR and initiatives from the wider QR organization

Workshops had two primary customer groupings in QR: the passenger group, who were under pressure from the state government to provide a steady increase in service outcomes for a steadily reducing quantity of public funding and with no reduction in safety; and the coal and freight group, who were under intense pressure to increase service levels simultaneously with a massive reduction in costs, again with no reduction in safety. The opening up of QR's network to third party operators meant that rail transport contracts were up for tender; and financial returns for the business, even if QR retained it, would be greatly reduced over what they had been in the past. For all transport operators in this sector margins were steadily decreasing, and pressure on cost management was growing ever more intense.

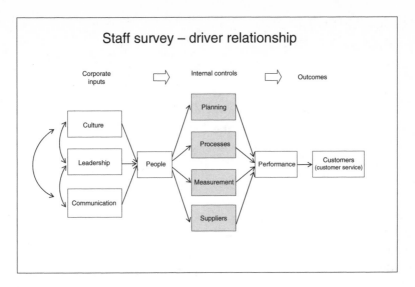

Figure CS.31 LISREL analysis of staff survey results

QR was determined to avoid the safety problems experienced by the southern railways, where the dissaggregation of inherently complex organizations such as rail, as a result of uncontrolled commercial pressures, had seen an increasing number of accidents. Workshops was an early step in the QR supply chain, and robust predictable process control was considered by Workshops management to be a critical part of the cost-reduction imperative if safety was not to be compromised.

The Workshops Excellence Six Sigma initiative

Thus, by the end of 2002, Six Sigma appeared to be the only process management and improvement methodology that met the major improvement requirements of the Workshops customer and staff surveys, the fundamental business improvement requirements of Workshops passenger and coal and freight customers and of a QR- wide initiative called 'Releasing QR's Potential'.

Six Sigma was selected as the appropriate improvement methodology for Workshops at this time for several reasons. Unlike total quality management (TQM), Six Sigma does not attempt to change the organization's culture; rather it redirects it. It builds upon the strong hierarchical structure of Workshops and utilizes the synergy within the organization.

Six Sigma is designed around utilizing natural workgroup teams, including the management of the teams. It creates vertical teams focused on a common purpose. It does not seek to empower without giving decision-making authority, as so often happened with TQM. There are clearly defined roles, including the traditional management roles. Leadership of business as usual is refocused onto leading for improvement of the business, in a structured and managed way. There are new tools and techniques drawn from a variety of disciplines that provide a shared common language with which to identify, analyse and resolve problems, and drive performance to improved levels through robust management and improvement of the work processes.

The implementation and structure of Workshops Excellence

In early 2003 the Workshops board of management (BOM) made the strategic decision to implement Six Sigma under the banner of 'Workshops Excellence', across all three sites simultaneously in a controlled top-down manner.

One of the strengths of Six Sigma is in the way it is embedded in sound management practice – in particular, locking down the responsibilities and accountabilities of leaders and managers. The Workshops GGM was keen to actively and visibly drive the Workshops Excellence initiative. In response to his question: 'How can I really get across this so that I can drive it properly?', the programme manager and consultant organized for half a day's training for the GGM in his role as executive champion prior to the presentation to the Workshops BOM. This enabled him to demonstrate visibly his support during the presentation, based on a firm foundation of knowledge and a basic foundation of skill.

Prior to the presentation to the BOM and the champion training, the Workshops Excellence programme manager redesigned position descriptions for managerial staff across the organization to lock down their responsibility for driving the Workshops Excellence initiative in their area of responsibility.

QR was developing performance agreements for all contract-level managers during this time, and the programme manager designed performance agreements that would effectively focus their efforts on their core responsibilities. This mechanism was designed to focus accountability on the Critical Few outcomes required of the managers. Those managers could then use the same style of writing performance outcomes in the performance agreements of their own direct reports. This mechanism was used to focus the effort of all onto the required outcomes for Workshops: productivity improvement, cost reduction and cycle time reduction through the Workshops Excellence Six Sigma programme, and the workplace reform that ran parallel with it.

In the performance agreements, measures were linked back to required business outcomes, for each key performance outcome. The outcome measures were a mix of soft (qualitative) and hard (quantitative) outcomes. They included the customer survey and staff satisfaction survey, specific items (questions) in both surveys and complete constructs (topics created from multiple items). One consequence of using the surveys in this way was the commitment to run the surveys yearly – previously they had only been run every second year. This approach was considerably more robust than the way performance agreements were traditionally handled, where outcomes (especially qualitative outcomes) were assessed on the basis of 'the boss's opinion' rather than independent data.

Traditionally bonuses are often tied to the financial outcomes and are weighted in favour of the financial components of performance agreements.

In Workshops the financial outcomes will be driven through the Workshops Excellence Six Sigma projects, based on achievable yet stretching targets that the managers commit to. This ensures numerator management rather than denominator management. In denominator management, budget reductions are achieved through downsizing staff numbers, cancelling or deferring maintenance programmes or reducing expenditure, with scant regard for their consequences on the sustainability of the organization or even the ongoing capability of the work processes to deliver the outcomes stated in business plans. If the reward and bonus process is not managed skilfully the risk is destruction of long-term organizational sustainability, as it is very easy to reduce expenditure on the areas that build competitive capability for the future. Numerator management is the preferred approach, where the organizational processes are systematically analysed and refined so that they deliver required outcomes in the most effective and efficient way for the long term.

For Workshops, as for other parts of QR, cost reduction is the critical challenge. It is of no value for Workshops customers, the external customer-facing business units, to be bringing in business that costs more to do than the revenue it provides. Competitive pressures mean that revenue streams will be substantially reduced; therefore, eliminating waste loss and rework is a critical imperative.

TIME FRAMES FOR THE IMPLEMENTATION

The Workshops Excellence initiative is anticipated to take at least two years – that is, two business planning cycles – to establish fully as part of the way Workshops drive and manage their process improvement from the business plan. It will take time for leaders to develop and consolidate their skills as the drivers of significant improvement projects using a strongly data-based analysis and decision process with tools that will be quite new to them.

There will also be a period of adjustment to re-focus their energies on driving improvement rather than overseeing

business as usual – 'getting product out the door'.

At the same time as the Workshops Excellence Six Sigma initiative rolls out, Workshops is commencing the visible and explicit use of the Australian Business Excellence Framework to drive improvement of all the management systems of the organization. As Six Sigma is the selected process improvement methodology of so many organizations, particularly in manufacturing, that have won equivalent awards around the world, this will provide a logical context for the Six Sigma drive.

ANTICIPATED IMPLEMENTATION PROBLEMS

It will be necessary to ensure the Workshops Excellence Black Belts and Workshops Excellence Green Belts are permitted the time to fulfil their roles. With Six Sigma, line managers along with their other normal full-time responsibilities drive the projects through their Black Belt role. Workshops, along with the wider QR, has a large number of initiatives running simultaneously and there is a risk that this might dilute effort from a critical responsibility.

The unwillingness of managers to reveal process deficiencies is anticipated to be a significant problem due to historical experience of seeing the punishment of bearers of bad news.

In addition, basic information systems are less sophisticated than those in other organizations, and are designed around government reporting responsibilities rather than the aim to provide managers with the management information required to run a business.

There are particular problems in relation

to 'quality' or 'process' data. Although large quantities of data are collected, they are generally not analysed effectively and certainly not for root cause analysis of faults. Therefore, the development of the basic building block on which Six Sigma is normally built has to be significantly fast-tracked in Workshops.

An issue emerging from the 2002 customer survey is the critical need to develop mechanisms for facilitating cooperation between Workshops and its customers in improving planning and streamlining the planning across several organizational boundaries. For example, Workshops needed to plan in detail significant jobs, such as the refurbishment of large numbers of locomotives. Sometimes expensive parts imported from overseas and involving long lead times are required, and advance planning is critical to reduce cycle times for jobs. The most frequent and significant hold-up for Workshops is unavailability of critical parts.

It is likely that Workshops' Six Sigma projects will need to include membership across several organizational boundaries for the projects to have any chance of success. The Workshops GGM has already initiated a cooperative project called the Alliance, which is providing a framework for service agreements between Workshops and one of its main customers who has committed to a partnership approach, so the environment is supportive for working together across boundaries.

The Workshops Excellence programme manager is using the network of quality professionals across the organization to seed interest in the benefits that Six Sigma can provide, and offering places on some courses to members of other quality teams throughout the organization where those

individuals will be members of Workshops teams for cross-functional projects. However, for Six Sigma to be effective it needs to be driven top-down, and other parts of QR will have to pick it up and implement it as a comprehensive process improvement methodology if problems are to be resolved effectively. Therefore the programme manager and external mentor will be delivering presentations to management teams across QR about the Workshops Excellence initiative in the early stages of the roll-out.

Strategic partners and consultants are also being trained so that the assistance they give on related projects will use the same language and a consistent approach. For example, Workshops utilize a measurement consultant to develop the measurement methodology to best practice consistent with the Business Excellence Framework and this person will be trained.

Resistance is expected from front-line managers, many of whom have been in their roles for a significant time, and may not all have in the past been held responsible for driving such comprehensive productivity improvement. Their perception of their responsibility is largely focused on 'getting production out the door'. The future need is for a broadening of capability for strategic focus.

The Workshops Excellence office is being established as a 'virtual team' with a Master Black Belt located on each of the three sites around the state in addition to the Workshops Excellence programme manager. It is anticipated that they will be very busy initially assisting and guiding the Black Belts.

At the time the Workshops Excellence initiative was being designed, Workshops was in the early stages of understanding the pros and cons of a gain sharing agreement for improving business performance, linked to a balanced scorecard.

In addition, a recognition programme is being designed to support the Workshops Excellence Six Sigma initiative.

Project selection

Projects are selected from the top down, based on the requirements of the Workshops strategic plan outcomes. The GGM has defined the improvement initiatives that are critical to achieving the Workshops plan outcomes. Each level of management will define their most critical, therefore highest priority improvement or cost-reduction requirements, and these will become their projects.

Other projects will be identified from an analysis of the quality system opportunities for improvement to identify commonly recurring and/or high impact faults affecting critical parts. Traction motors and wheel sets are such critical parts.

Selection of Workshops Excellence Six Sigma staff

Workshops Excellence Six Sigma staff are selected on two criteria:

- their hierarchical position, which places them in a specific role with specific responsibilities for Six Sigma and
- their ability to meet strict selection criteria.

All Six Sigma staff will be selected from within QR, and the majority from within Workshops Group itself.

The divisional managers who report to the GGM Workshops are all trained as champions, and their position descriptions and performance agreements reflect those responsibilities. The next level down, called operations managers, are all trained as Workshops Excellence Black Belts, and their responsibilities for driving Workshops Excellence projects is again captured in their position descriptions and performance agreements.

In addition, the senior quality personnel within the business improvement division, and the senior quality personnel on each of the three sites, are trained as Master Black Belts because their positions are integral to the Workshops Excellence initiative as it rolls out, and the Six Sigma training is vital to developing them for their new role.

A range of other staff in specialist positions are to be trained as Black Belts and they will be selected according to their potential ability as set against the capability requirements of the Black Belt role profile. Although they are to be taught all Six Sigma tools and techniques, their potential capability to fulfil the organization development role, to work with initiative and to adapt to change and handle the intellectual challenge of the Black Belt role will be assessed at selection stage.

The same selection process will be used for Workshops Excellence Green Belts, who will be part-time initially. The skills developed in these and the Workshops Excellence Black Belt roles will become critical to meeting the requirements of future leadership roles in the organization.

Training of Workshops Excellence Six Sigma staff

The Workshops Excellence Six Sigma

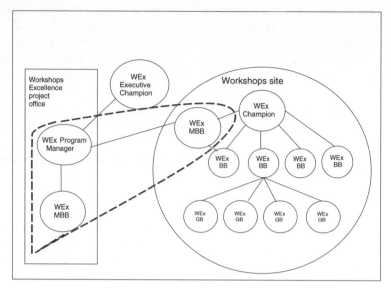

Figure CS.3m   Workshops Excellence structure

initiative was designed in partnership with an external mentor from a university and the QR Workshops business improvement manager who established and managed the Workshops Excellence office.

The external mentor carries out the training of the Executive Champion and Champions and the initial group of Master Black Belts, which includes the business improvement manager. From then on these two will train all subsequent Black Belts and Green Belts. A significant number of Black Belts and Green Belts will be trained to take account of the likely attrition levels and loss to other parts of QR through promotions. An integral part of the change strategy is to manage the culture change through saturating the entire Workshops organization with a common language, methodology and toolset for process improvement, and to lock that in to HR structures, specifically selection and performance management. The establishment of Yellow and White Belt levels is also under consideration. Other development initiatives will be designed, as required, to foster creativity, innovation and skill in exploring and identifying new options for process management.

QR Workshops has a history of driving corporate initiatives through to success, having already made a significant culture change through wide and deep implementation of two linked courses called 'Getting on Track' and 'Workshops on Track'. These have been used to significantly improve staff focus on customer needs. Workshops is the only part of QR that has implemented these courses with a sufficient number of staff to achieve the outcomes they were designed to deliver.

The Workshops Excellence initiative training will be approached in the same way.

During the early phase the external mentor will fulfil the role of Master Black Belt. This role will be gradually handed over to the Workshops business improvement manager. The Workshops Excellence office is run by this manager as a 'virtual team', with site representatives taking stronger roles as they develop their competency, so aspects of what is traditionally the Master Black Belt role are to be shared over time. This is consistent with QR Workshops' strategy to develop a coaching culture throughout the organization.

There will be a mix of full-time and part-time roles in the Workshops Excellence structure; the exact mix will be developed as the initiative evolves.

Workshops Excellence project reviews

The Workshops Excellence projects will be reviewed every three months on a rolling schedule. This process will be driven by Workshops Excellence programme manager, and by the team of Master Black Belts at site level.

The Workshops Excellence programme manager will provide rolling reviews to the Workshops BOM at the monthly meeting.

Project savings will be measured by:

- financial formulae and estimates
- customer survey ratings.

Benefits will be measured by:

- customer survey ratings and comments
- staff survey ratings and comments.

QR Workshops and the wider QR organization use several other improvement strategies:

- Australian Business Excellence Framework (Workshops and selected other QR divisions only)
- ISO 9001/Quality Assurance
- project management
- strategy mapping
- balanced scorecard.

Workshops Excellence Role	Responsibility	Organizational position with prime responsibility	Full or part time
Executive Champion	Drives the initiative as the accepted productivity improvement and process improvement methodology for the Group. Models decision process.	GGM Workshops.	P/T
Champion	Oversees improvement projects in their area of responsibility – this may be for an end to end process, or sub-process.	General managers.	P/T
Workshops Excellence Program Manager	Manages the WEx Initiative/WE Office; design program, adapt program to the existing culture, designs and drives culture change to support productivity improvement and process management, manages training, guides succession/career path of WEx professionals. Mentors Executive Champion.	Business improvement manager.	F/T
Master Black Belt	Mentors Champions. Guides Black Belts. Provides expertise in statistics, change facilitation, group process, tool selection.	High level quality professionals.	F/T
Black Belt	Drives the project. Manages the team, particularly cross-functional teams. Takes responsibility for the project outcomes.	Operations managers and other managers at same level. Selected others.	P/T
Green Belt	Drives small, less complex projects. Manages small teams. Participates as member on significant projects. Collects and analyses data.	Open to all staff (subject to selection process, and organizational need).	Mix F/T and P/T

Figure CS.3n   Workshops Excellence roles

The integration of Six Sigma with other improvement programmes and systems

Workshops Excellence Six Sigma initiative is QR Workshops' selected process improvement methodology under Category 6, 'Processes, products and services', in the Australian Business Excellence Framework; and it will provide the 'in-process' and 'process outcome' measures for Category 3, 'Data information and knowledge'. The linkages will be made transparent to all staff as the Business Excellence Framework awareness progresses through Workshops.

Workshops Excellence is also the overarching methodology for Workshops to deliver both productivity outcomes of the Workshops strategy map and the productivity improvement targets in the balanced scorecard, and for driving the process improvements identified in the 'Process' section of the Workshops strategy map.

The 'in-process' and 'process outcome' measures delivered by the Workshops Excellence projects will be the driver measures that link to the Workshops balanced scorecard process and financial measures.

The Workshops Excellence improvement plans are linked to the Workshops strategy map, which is in turn linked to the wider QR strategy map.

Rewards for Workshops Excellence Six Sigma staff

There is at this stage no intention to make experience in driving successful Workshops Excellence projects mandatory for being considered for future leadership roles in QR, but the reality is that the job of leader at all levels in Workshops is being redefined as the driver of change and of organizational performance improvement. The reality is that demonstrated skill in utilizing Six Sigma to bring about these improvements provides an enormous competitive edge for people with experience in implementing Workshops Excellence when they apply for leadership positions.

One of the beneficial outcomes for Workshops was anticipated as being the identification and training of future leadership talent. Selection for Six Sigma roles was to be a cornerstone of the succession management process, particularly in identifying latent leadership talent from the workforce that would not have been evident through previous mechanisms.

One of the biggest threats to retaining enough Six Sigma trained staff to maintain the Workshops Excellence initiative during its implementation is the risk of losing them to other parts of QR or external industry. Workshops is committed to making a significant investment in identifying and developing staff who would be able to perform well in the role, and, once they had some experience under their belt they would be very attractive to poach – both into quality improvement and leadership roles.

Six Sigma in the Customer Service Industry

Mr H.S. Kim
Samsung Everland, Korea

Introduction

The following case study is about the implementation of Six Sigma at Samsung Everland, Korea, a leisure and recreation park operating in a typical customer service environment. It is a brief summary of Everland's relentless pursuit of customer service excellence during the past ten years. In this case study, effort has been made to highlight the specific characteristics of the Six Sigma deployment process chosen by Samsung Everland.

The company

Established in 1963, the company currently employs more than 1700 people. Its operations includes five major business sectors:

- food and beverage distribution
- building engineering and management
- resort complex development and management
- environment development and management and
- golf course management.

Everland is the largest outdoor amusement park in Korea, comprising three major elements: 'Festival World', 'Caribbean Bay' and 'Everland Speedway'. Festival World boasts some 40 modern attractions, the world's only multiplex wildlife park, year-round flower festivals and a snow-sleigh park; Caribbean Bay is a world-class indoor/outdoor water theme-park; Everland Speedway provides safe motor racing opportunity for Koreans. Together they offer an extraordinary variety of attractions and events for people of all ages.

In addition to the three parks, Everland is equipped with accommodation facilities for 1300 people, the Ho-Am Art Museum, an automobile museum, a banquet hall, two training facilities where Service Academy and Cooking Academy's lectures are regularly held, a nine-hole public golf course and a golf practising range. There is also a 49 000-pyong playground (one pyong is equal to 3.3 square metres).

Samsung Everland's business philosophy, as shown in Figure CS.4a, has always been a simple one: 'Creating the time and space for the human spirit' (*samgan* is the Korean word for 'spirit'). Its continual emphasis on excellent customer service has won the company several awards, including:

- the Customer Satisfaction Business Award Grand Prize for Customer Satisfaction for five consecutive years from 1996 to 2000

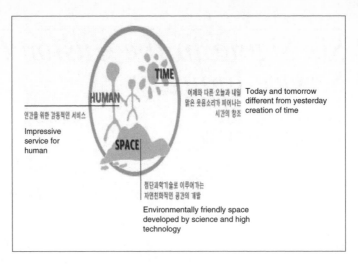

Figure CS.4a   Samsung Everland's business philosophy

- *Maeil Business Newspaper* – Booze Allen Knowledge Management Award Grand Prize in 2000.

The adoption of Six Sigma

Samsung Everland's management innovation is based on the principle that stronger competitiveness will be achieved through the differentiation and discrimination of its products, services and processes. Its management style is based on continuous change and innovation (see Figure CS.4b).

In 1994, the company focused on customer satisfaction, environmental safety and design management through friendliness of services, cleanliness of premises, informatization,* provision of luxury products, globalization and safety. In the following years, Samsung Everland has announced an era of knowledge management and Six Sigma implementation in order to further improve business performance.

*Informatization: the application of information technology to the business processses.

As with many other companies, Samsung Everland used a top-down approach for the implementation of Six Sigma. To start the Six Sigma implementation process, top management announced the policy that stronger competitiveness means differentiation and discrimination of products, services and processes. In accordance with this policy, the top management has invited everyone in the company to participate.

According to the management, it wasn't particularly important whether this could be achieved by the implementation of a programme called Six Sigma: what was more important was that the company was using tools and techniques which would deliver better results than the competition. Only after lengthy discussions was it decided that Six Sigma was the most suitable programme currently available to achieve the company's goals and objectives.

One of the main reasons for implementing Six Sigma was not only that it was an innovative management programme but it was also being used by many of the world's leading organizations. While the main

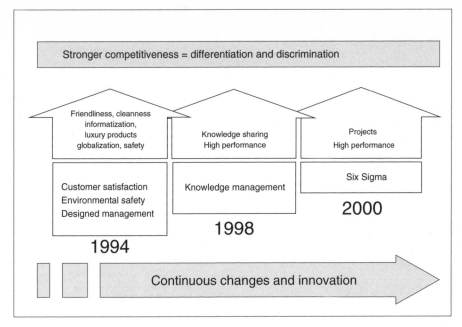

Figure CS.4b   Continuous change and innovation process. Designed management = Planned management

goal for Six Sigma implementation was 'the achievement of top-class competitiveness', four areas were identified as the core objectives of the Six Sigma deployment (Figure CS.4c). These were:

1. education and training
2. internal process innovation (process improvement)
3. customer satisfaction and
4. financial results.

Today, Six Sigma is the central point of Samsung Everland's business model which combines management philosophy, work methods and the innovation strategy.

The innovation strategy involves developing products, services and processes to secure world-class competitiveness. While the management philosophy is based on customers and their expectations, the work method component of the model refers to decision-making based on data and measurement.

The Six Sigma deployment process

As depicted in Figure CS.4d, Samsung Everland's Six Sigma implementation process consists of five stages and the overall journey is expected to take four to five years:

- Preparation for Six Sigma deployment (1999–2000)
- Introduction (2000)
- Expansion (2001)
- Establishment (2002) and
- Stabilization (2004–05).

During the 'Preparation' phase, top managers including the CEO and executives were trained to understand Six Sigma deployment requirements. With the help of an external consultancy firm a master plan was developed at this stage.

In the 'Introduction' phase, Six Sigma was introduced to the whole company by explaining the reasons behind the decision

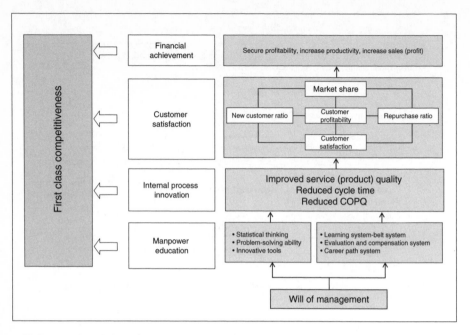

Figure CS.4c   Goal and objectives of the Six Sigma deployment

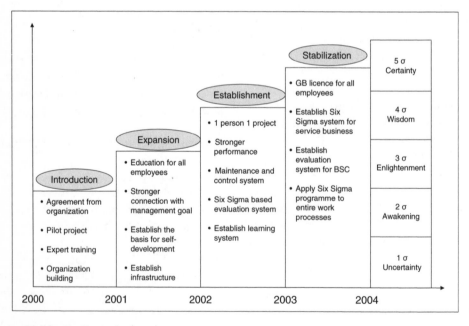

Figure CS.4d   Six Sigma deployment process

why Six Sigma was chosen for continuous improvement. This phase also included the training of some experts, the building of a Six Sigma foundation and the completion of several pilot projects.

During the 'Expansion' phase, Six Sigma was rolled out to the rest of the company which included a stronger linkage of the Six Sigma methodology with management goals and objectives, education of all employees and establishment of a Six Sigma infrastructure.

The 'Establishment' phase helped to complete the deployment process of the Six Sigma methodology within the organization. Some of the characteristics of this phase included the establishment of a performance maintenance and control system, a learning and training system and a Six Sigma based evaluation system.

The final, 'Stabilization' phase was required to make Six Sigma an essential part of management's daily activities. It was also envisaged to provide Green Belt training to all employees, establishment of an

evaluation system for BSC and use of Six Sigma in the entire service business.

Aligning the Six Sigma project with company goals

One of the main benefits of using Six Sigma for process improvement was the fact that Six Sigma projects were aligned with Samsung Everland's goals and objectives. As illustrated in Figure CS.4e, the company's four core objectives – 'Customer satisfaction', 'Employee education and training', 'Process improvement' and 'Financial results' – were used as key criteria for identification of the CTQs at business level. This level consists of the core business functions including the main and support processes. Where necessary, CTQs have been broken down further to the operational and sub-process levels.

The Six Sigma infrastructure

One of the essential requirements of the Six Sigma deployment process at Samsung

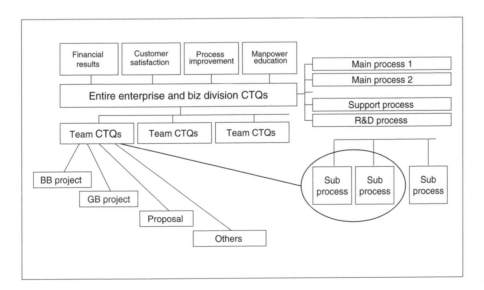

Figure CS.4e   Aligning Six Sigma projects with the company goals and objectives

Everland was that the infrastructure had to be clearly defined before the programme was rolled out in the organization. This infrastructure included the roles and responsibilities of the different competency levels (Belts) and the other positions (such as champion, department head and financial analyst) involved in the Six Sigma implementation process (Figure CS.4f).

Six Sigma Projects

Figure CS.4g shows the typical Six Sigma project flow diagram used by Everland. First, projects are selected by the champion and process owner using the CTQs identified in the alignment process. A project plan is then defined by Black Belts and Green Belts by taking into account all the other requirements, including resource availability, urgency or improvement and customer and financial impact. The next step is the approval of a project by the champion and process owner. The approval process may require some changes to be made to the project plan. Once the project has been approved, Black Belts and Green Belts will implement the project according to the plan which usually takes three to five months.

Each project is then evaluated by the Six Sigma office to assess whether it has achieved the planned project goal or not. This also helps to complete the Black Belt and Green Belt certification process. After the training, Black Belts and Green Belts usually receive a certificate of attendance. In the case of the satisfactory completion of a project, the final certification (licence) will be issued to the Black Belt and Green Belt involved in the project.

The Six Sigma office monitors the performance of the various Belts and reports

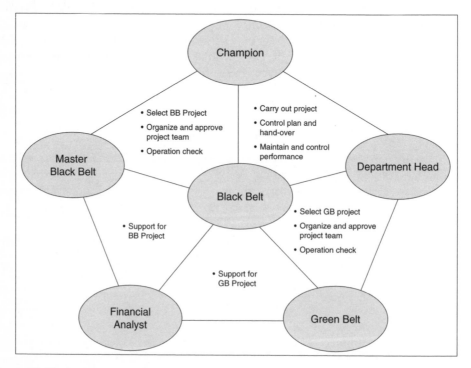

Figure CS.4f   Six Sigma infrastructure

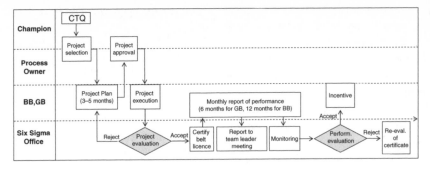

Figure CS.4g   Six Sigma project flow chart and Belt certification process

the results to the team leader meeting at regular intervals. The report usually also includes a performance evaluation, which either recommends a monetary reward or the re-evaluation of the licence for the Black Belt and Green Belt.

Six Sigma training

At Samsung Everland, the typical champion training is conducted in one week, while the training of the Black Belts and Green Belts takes much longer to complete: around three to six months.

The entire Black Belt training is usually conducted over six months in order to allow sufficient time for each of the five steps of a typical Six Sigma project. Every month during their training period, Black Belts receive one week's training. Immediately after the training sessions, they apply learned skills and knowledge to their assigned project. At the end of the training, they are also required to present their completed project.

Green Belt training takes usually up to three months. First, prospective Green Belts receive three days' training. In the following two months, they apply learned skills and knowledge to their projects. At the end of their training programme, they receive another three days' training and present their project results.

At Samsung Everland, the different Six Sigma competency levels (Green Belt, Black Belt and Master Black Belt) have been used to create a whole new learning system. Some of the key issues associated with this learning system have been identified and addressed as follows:

- How to improve the efficiency of the learning outcomes for all competency levels
  - Develop more user-friendly manuals and tools. This was addressed at the Master Black Belt meetings usually conducted at the end of each month
  - Enhance the Master Black Belt's ability to conduct more efficient lectures and to instruct projects. This was achieved by developing sample lectures
  - Increase the exchange of knowledge and expertise with external companies
  - Develop Design For Six Sigma (DFSS) materials and train experts in advance by using external consultants.

- How to consolidate roles of the Master Black Belt and Black Belt as education leaders
  - The role of the Master Black Belt will change to Six Sigma consultant after two years of practical experience
  - The Master Black Belt will increase expertise through experience in diverse roles (for example, planning, expansion,

performance management, education, instruction, methodology development)
- The Black Belt role is established as a full-time position. The certification process and functional roles have been separated
- The Master Black Belt and Black Belt will be rewarded for contributions to research and development
- Quarterly Black Belt workshops will be held to expand best practices.

• How to encourage active participation by using the performance evaluation system
- Certification will be cancelled if the performance is poor in the activity evaluation. Evaluation items include: project performance, Belt education and project instruction.

SIX SIGMA COMPETENCY-BASED EVALUATION SYSTEM

The typical characteristics of the Six Sigma competency-based performance evaluation system include:

• Stricter conditions for Belt licences
- approval by champion and process owner
- pilot test
- certification and evaluation after implementation

• The establishment of a maintenance and control system for project performance
- monthly report of project performance
- and regular report to team leader meeting
- monitoring of the entire company (biannually)
- the early establishment of post-management system through Sigma Park and efficiency improvement
- performance evaluation criteria (financial, non-financial)
- evaluator training.

Improvements under Six Sigma

One of the early signs of culture change initiated by Six Sigma implementation was that Samsung Everland began to approach business matters using Six Sigma tools and methods. Employees at every level started to realize that Six Sigma was the appropriate programme to enable them to deliver process improvement outcomes. However, in the early stages, Six Sigma was mainly applied to solve problems that had already occurred in the processes. It was predominantly a reactive approach to problem-solving.

At the later stages of Six Sigma deployment, managers and staff started to use Six Sigma as an effective and systematic way of generating ideas for business improvement as well. One of the specific requirements of Everland's Six Sigma programme was that decisions were not to be made on the basis of gut feeling. Managers were required to consider data and facts when making business decisions. This was not only useful to educate managers and change their working methods, but it also helped to lower the risk associated with the decisions and reduce losses caused by incorrect decisions.

Culture change is a long-term process. People don't change their behaviours overnight. At Everland, the initial Six Sigma implementation stage took around three years. One of the key results achieved at this stage was that employees from all levels started to participate in process improvements. This was mainly achieved through the typical Black Belt and Green Belt activities. The number of employees being trained in Six Sigma Belts and their involvement in process improvement is constantly increasing.

Currently, Samsung Everland is in the last stage of its Six Sigma implementation process and is stabilizing the gains made throughout the organization. Whether hard or soft savings, Six Sigma deployment helped Everland achieve more than 3 billion Korean Won (around US$ 2.5m) cost savings in its operations in the past three years.

Six Sigma is currently also being used for expansion of the business into new markets. Most importantly, Samsung Everland is using Six Sigma as the core engine for management innovation to drive its cultural transformation.

Six Sigma in the Banking Business

Dr Uwe H. Kaufmann and Ms Amy Tan Bee Choo
AON, Singapore

Introduction

'Six Sigma does not work for my business.'
'It is for manufacturing processes only.'
'Are you sure you can use statistics to analyse our processes or implement control charts to monitor the people's behaviour?'

These have been some of the common remarks one of the authors received when invited to spearhead and deploy Six Sigma strategy for a bank in Europe in the late 1990s. To many people, Six Sigma is about tangible data analysis and it will seem inappropriate to apply it in the service industries. People experience fear when Six Sigma is proposed or commences implementation, but this is mainly due to the misconceptions of associating it with a heavily mathematical and statistical approach to problem-solving or process improvement. In this case study, we will look at how a bank successfully adopted and implemented Six Sigma as one of its management tools.

OurBank

OurBank is an American international bank with 50 branches in Germany and staff strength of approximately 300 employees working either in the head office or in one of the branches.

The company decided to adopt and implement Six Sigma during their annual corporate leadership strategic meeting. It was intended that Six Sigma would be deployed as the primary business management improvement tool across all business units in Europe. The high-level deployment plan was agreed as follows:

- a senior management workshop
- Black Belt training
- project work.

Senior management workshop to define improvement projects

The two-day senior management workshop was intended to give the OurBank management team an overview of Six Sigma as well as some real practical applications using the statistical tools and methodology. It was also intended to make those managers, who would potentially be the sponsors of the business projects, aware of what would be expected from them.

The workshop was designed with

practical exercises through simulation role-play. The simulation exercise was called 'Move It™'. In this exercise delegates work in different teams and in the roles required to prepare and deliver mail packages to their customers. Delegates immersed themselves in the simulation experience in the roles of workers in the Move It courier company. They went through the process of sorting and preparing mail packages and in meeting customers' expectations. Through the simulation, delegates learnt to apply the basic Six Sigma methodology to improve the courier service and overall delivery cycle time as well as reduce defect rates.

Comments from managers and leaders who went through the simulation were mostly very positive. They appreciated the need for such a learning intervention, and the simulation revealed how, by using a simple process improvement methodology, they could produce significant effectiveness and efficiency improvements that impacted on business results. Besides learning the basics of Six Sigma, one foundation stone was laid in preparing the organization for the Six Sigma roll-out: the deployment strategy was agreed. This included some of the critical issues such as:

- What is the business management strategy today?
- What are some of the most important or critical business issues that have an impact on business and need to be addressed?
- Who are the people likely to be involved?

A well designed implementation or deployment strategy is required to ensure all management staff are fully engaged and committed. One of the critical success factors of implementing Six Sigma is whether staff at all levels and customers are all involved in process improvement.

'To fail to prepare is to prepare to fail'

During the senior management workshop, OurBank went through thorough discussion on their business strategy and identified the car loan business as one of their business priorities in the next two years. The strategy was to penetrate the market by growing their car loan business market share within the region in two years' time. The car loan business growth plan seemed quite aggressive. There were some doubts amongst the management about whether Six Sigma could really help to achieve the target. Some of the typical concerns included:

'We are not talking about defects or complaints.'
'We are talking about business development. In what way will "Quality" be able to support this strategy?'

More than half of the leadership team recommended not using Six Sigma to support this business strategy due to the level of risk associated with it. Such a situation was almost expected, particularly for OurBank; since there had been only a few success stories with Six Sigma in the banking and service industries prior to that time. However, at the end of the two-day senior management workshop, the team came to a compromise and made a decision on adopting Six Sigma in the car loan business. The decision was made to form a team with staff members from and across different functions (sales, marketing and operations) to look into how to grow the car loan business and hence increase the market share. It was also decided to appoint one of the sales representatives, who was also considered to be one of their best high potentials, to be the Black Belt.

One of the challenges the team faced initially was identifying the barriers to the existing car loan business. However, to do this, the team needed to examine and understand the entire car loan business, which was achieved with the help of the team sponsor (sales director).

Figure CS.5a shows the top level car loan process and the initial identified problems from the management perspective. However, to tackle the whole car loan process seemed to be too broad and unlikely to lead to immediate financial results for OurBank. The other difficulty which the team faced was supporting the project with process measurements. This might be an easy task in a manufacturing process but it is more difficult in a banking or service environment. Hence the team, supported by the sponsor, reviewed the process in more detail by looking into sub-processes so as to narrow the scope of the project and, at the same time, identify the process measurements and specific issues.

Pre-analysis to identify business indicators

The team developed a top-level process map to identify the sub-processes and the relevant drivers belonging to the sub-processes that in turn drove the car loan business turnover (Figure CS.5b). The process mapping was not too difficult since the banking processes had previously been mapped for inclusion in the operational manual. The identification of the indicators was simply a series of interviews with the process stakeholders. They did not know about process indicators but they were able to express what kind of 'critical numbers' they look at monthly. Some of those numbers were translated into indicators easily. Some of the indicators needed more work to make them visible and usable.

It was not an easy job to identify all the indicators, and it was even more difficult to obtain some information about the baseline for some of the indicators. This was

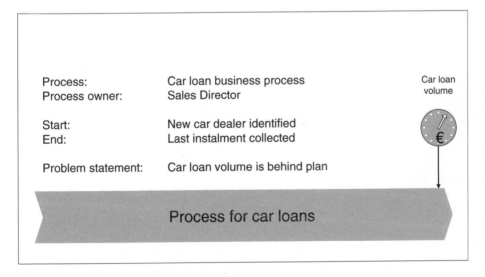

Process:	Car loan business process
Process owner:	Sales Director
Start:	New car dealer identified
End:	Last instalment collected
Problem statement:	Car loan volume is behind plan

Car loan volume

Process for car loans

Figure CS.5a   High-level problem statement

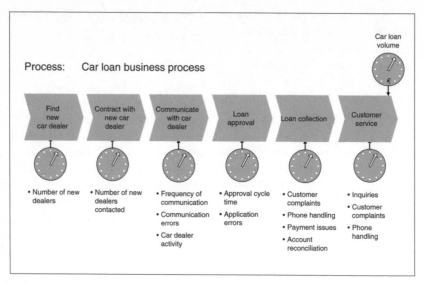

Figure CS.5b   Pre-analysis to identify business indicators

addressed in a second series of interviews when the team had clarified exactly what to ask for. In spite of the great effort put in at the start, the team was not progressing well. One of the frustrations they expressed was that the entire process was enormous and it was critical that the respective sub-process owners contributed to pinpoint the specific problem areas (Figure CS.5c). This is not unusual; this type of situation occurs very often in Six Sigma projects. Finally the team identified two Black Belt and two Green Belt projects (Figure CS.5d). The distinction between Black Belt and Green Belt was not made because of the difficulty of the task for which they were appointed; it was mainly decided depending on the urgency of the

task, in the hope that full-time Black Belts would be able to deal with the problem faster and more effectively than part-time Green Belts.

The project definition

The final project definition for one of the Black Belt projects had a narrow scope including only one sub-process: communication with car dealers (Figure CS.5e). One of the reasons for starting this project was common sense: it was recognized after the interviews and after extracting some data from the management information system that more than half of

Sub-process	Voice of the process owner	Process indicator
Find new car dealer	'Number of new car dealers'	Number of new car dealers/month
Communication with car dealer	'We must care about them'	Number of contacts/month
	'No errors'	Number of complaints from car dealers
	'They should generate business'	% inactive car dealers
Loan collection	'Phone handling is important'	% abandoned calls, Speed of answer in seconds

Figure CS.5c   Examples for process indicators

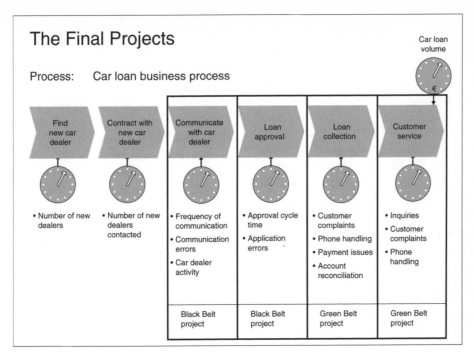

Figure CS.5d   Identifying the final projects

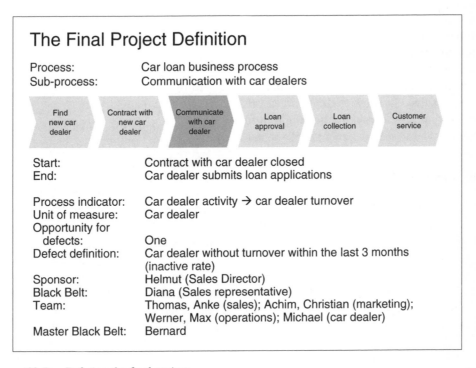

Figure CS.5e   Defining the final project

the car dealers had not done any business over the last couple of months. The definition for the defect emerged as: 'All car dealers who have not made any turnover during a three-month period are seen as "defective"'.

Common sense together with some marketing data told the team that it was much more expensive (about 500 per cent) to acquire new car dealers than to work with existing ones. One of the biggest obstacles faced at the point of forming the team was engaging the process owner in the project. The car loan business process owner, who was the sales director, was one of the few who had some scepticism about Six Sigma. Therefore the team at the beginning was not committed at all.

The other obstacle was to bring the sales, marketing and operations departments together, and this was a challenge due to the fact that they were situated in two different locations. The three departments had not been communicating regularly in the past, so there was a great difficulty in kicking off the first project team meeting. Despite the teething issues at the beginning of team formation, the Master Black Belt did an excellent job in influencing the team, especially process owner, by helping him to understand and see the benefit of Six Sigma.

LESSONS LEARNED

- Right from the beginning you need to show that Six Sigma is an imperative that contributes to the strategy of the company
- Show the need for the Six Sigma projects rather than starting some 'training projects' with the intention to learn about Six Sigma
- Make sure you organize the buy-in of the senior management first.

The voice of the customer is key

During interviews carried out to identify business indicators and to determine their baseline, the team experienced a very common opinion expressed by sales staff: 'We could make more turnover if we had better conditions'. This is never a surprise in any business in the world. The team decided as part of the measure phase to explore the voice of the customer even more. The team designed – supported by an external market research company – a client survey that was carried out via phone with about 130 car dealers (Figure CS.5f). The result was a big surprise:

- 60 per cent of the interviewees mentioned non-existent or poor communication with the bank as the biggest driver for dissatisfaction
- for about 20 per cent, the interest rate for the car loans seemed to be too high.

During the analysis phase the team focused on those two issues. They went through the process of communication between the sales team and the clients. Surprisingly enough they had to recognize that there was *no* process. The sales representatives complained about the workload they had to do every day. They were kept busy by preparing reports, making sales presentations and attending a lot of internal meetings. They did not really focus on talking to their clients. 'If I have some time left I give my clients a call' was one of the typical comments. Or: 'They closed the contract. Do I need to chase them any longer?' Unfortunately the contract was a frame contract, non-exclusive, not binding at all. Clients could decide to get the loan for their car customers from OurBank or from someone else. The analysis of the interest rate did bring up an additional issue that was

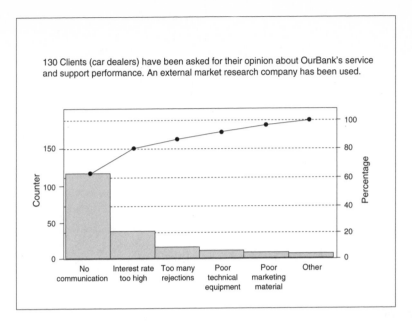

130 Clients (car dealers) have been asked for their opinion about OurBank's service and support performance. An external market research company has been used.

Figure CS.5f   Client survey results

even worse: the team was surprised to discover that some of the clients did not know the newly reduced interest rate of OurBank that had been published weeks ago.

After further analysis the root cause for this serious fault was exposed as the communication channel between marketing and operations not working very well. Immediate action was taken to inform all clients about the better rate.

LESSONS LEARNED

- Don't assume you know what the customers want. Ask them
- Six Sigma goals should be derived from the business situation and should be anchored in client satisfaction
- Six Sigma goals often focus solely on cost reduction. They should be incorporating both top-line growth and cost reduction
- Six Sigma is not about bureaucracy even if it has a very rigid way of ensuring that the methodology and the tools are applied appropriately. In case of findings

pinpointing obvious process problems, quick fixes are allowed if there is no risk for other processes
- Six Sigma is not about blaming people even if you see 'unbelievable' weaknesses. People are not the problem. Fix the process and allow the people to do their jobs unhindered.

Implementing solutions and sustaining the gain

A couple of days after the market research company contacted OurBank's clients the turnover produced by the former 'sleeping clients' went up. The team was surprised again. The process had not been touched but the results started to improve (Figure CS.5g).

One of the underlying reasons for that surprising improvement on the business performance was due to the customer satisfaction survey phone calls. It created a perception among the car dealers that OurBank valued them as priority clients.

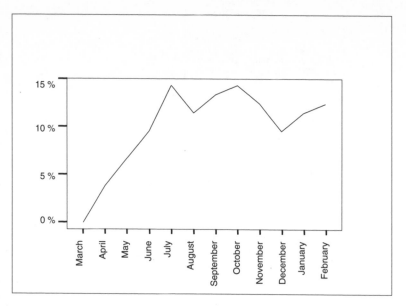

Figure CS.5g   Increase of car dealer turnover from 'sleeping dealers'

Another reason for business growth was the communication of the new rates, which were more aggressive and competitive. All in all, the senior management gained some confidence in the Six Sigma approach having shown some good first results. Voices like 'Do you really need Six Sigma to figure out those obvious things?' did not really get a lot of support. The buy-in for the next step was gained. The Six Sigma team, led by the Black Belt, met to develop solutions for addressing the main problem root causes:

- the development of a communication process between sales representatives and clients
- the development of a monitoring tool to alert sales at the exact time when clients became inactive
- the refinement of the roles of marketing, sales and operations resulting in removing some administration work from the sales force in order to give them the chance for their first priority: talking to the clients
- the redefinition of internal interfaces to

improve communication between departments
- the layout of a marketing handbook to support clients selling OurBank's services.

The presence and support of one of the clients, a car dealer, was essential, especially during the improve phase. He gave the important input about how often and how he would like to be contacted by the sales force. He was the one who drafted most of the marketing handbook.

The solutions needed some investments. During a project presentation in the company's Six Sigma steering team meeting, the Black Belt and his team proposed the solutions and asked for the sign-off to spend some money on the process improvement. Obtaining the approval was easier than the team had previously thought. The major differentiator were the data about the additional turnover and about the decrease of the process indicator – the rate of inactive car dealers – they could show. They used the data to extrapolate the growth for a one-year period and compared these data with the

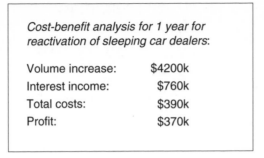

Cost-benefit analysis for 1 year for
reactivation of sleeping car dealers:

Volume increase:	$4200k
Interest income:	$760k
Total costs:	$390k
Profit:	$370k

Figure CS.5h   Cost-benefit analysis of reactivation of 'sleeping dealers'

costs expected for the solution (Figure CS.5h). The sales director was 100 per cent supportive of the solution.

Part of this phase included:

- communication with the whole organization
- describing the new process in the (so-called) operational manual
- training all people involved in the process on the changes.

The consecutive project phase control was about putting mechanisms in place to make sure that the process improvements lasted. Part of control was to make the 'inactive rate' part of the company's management information system, showing the actual inactive rate monthly so that action could be taken if it deviated from the 'norm' (Figure CS.5i).

To decide whether a deviation was critical or not, the team implemented a control chart. The control chart was built using the weekly inactive rate once the process was stabilized over a period of one quarter after implementing the changes.

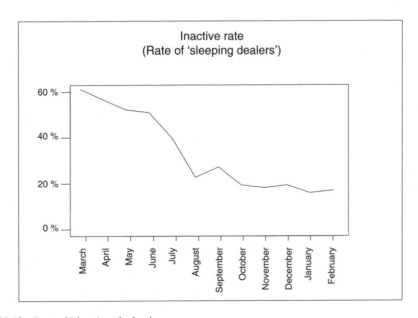

Figure CS.5i   Rate of 'sleeping dealers'

Using a control chart for such purposes seems to be questionable as such charts are often used for a typical manufacturing process. The team decided to use this tool to monitor the variation in the improved process. It helped the team to distinguish between a typical pattern and abnormalities in this process.

LESSONS LEARNED

- Measuring the process implies changing the behaviour of the people. Measuring the right indicators implies changing the behaviour in the right direction. You will see some improvements shortly after having started the data collection. But don't assume this improvement will stay for longer than you measure unless you implement some tools that help sustain that gain
- Involving clients in project work could be a challenge as it can put the company at risk in exposing potential intellectual or proprietary information. The key to manage this is to establish a trust-based relationship so as to achieve win–win outcomes
- The use of control charts in a service type of process is recommended, provided it is defined correctly at the beginning. The process owner must also understand the purpose as well as the usage, and the most important thing is utilizing the results to aid any relevant changes to the process.

Summary

After the changes recommended by the team were implemented and after the results became obvious Six Sigma experienced increasing momentum within the company. The start of further Six Sigma projects did not depend any longer on the push by the head office but became more and more part of the normal business. The sales director did show his newly gained commitment by proposing 'his' Six Sigma team for a reward and recognition event in the head office of the enterprise.

The results in addition to the profit made from this project were:

- OurBank gained very valueable information about the voice of the clients and their needs as well as the impact of internal processes upon that
- the team experienced the power of teamwork, communication and process analysis rather than application of complex statistical tools
- additional improvement opportunities had been identified during the project work which resulted in a restructuring of the client's communication process in other business areas.

Implementing Six Sigma in the banking business does make a lot of sense.

Glossary

The Australian Business Excellence Framework (ABEF)
Established in 1987, the ABEF consists of 12 principles and 7 categories which provide the assessment model for the Australian Business Excellence Awards.

Accuracy
The numerical difference between measurements that are taken, and an accepted standard. The smaller the difference, the more accurate is the measured value.

Attribute
A quality characteristic that can be measured as either conforming or nonconforming to defined specifications. Typical decisions involve Yes or No, Go or No go and Pass or Fail.

Average
The average, also referred to as the 'mean' is the arithmetic value obtained when the sum of all observations are divided by the total number of observations.

Black Belt
A competency-based Six Sigma qualification level. Black Belts are typically required to have managerial skills, including people and project management skills, as they usually act as leaders of Six Sigma projects.

Business Excellence Framework
A model that is used to define a set of criteria for organizational self-assessment against agreed best practice generic organizational management systems and the basis for judging entrants to a (national or international) quality award scheme.

Business Process Management (BPM)
A concept or approach used to better manage and improve business processes. Most BPM models consist of several aspects, including the human aspect, the information aspect and the process aspect. BPM and Six Sigma share similar process management or improvement tools and methods.

Cause
A factor that has a negative or a positive impact on an outcome.

Cause-and-effect (CE) diagram
The CE diagram, also referred to as the Fishbone or Ishikawa diagram, is a graphic display of the relationship between an outcome and the factors which have a negative or positive impact on that outcome.

Champion
A Six Sigma level that is typically assigned to a senior manager or head of a division who is responsible for Six Sigma implementation in the division or department. Champions are involved in the project selection and reviews, and provide resources for training and support project teams.

Check sheet
A commonly used and simple tool that helps collect and record data.

Common cause (of variation)
The reason for or source of failure that is part of the whole system or inherent in the process itself. Its occurrence is periodic, random or predictable.

Continuous data
In contrast to discrete data, which can only take on discrete (fixed or exact) values, continuous data can take on any value. For instance, measuring the weight or height of people can produce any value on the scale.

Control chart
A graphic display with statistically determined upper and lower limits for monitoring trends of a process. It also helps identifying causes of changes (variation) within the process.

Control limits
Statistically calculated boundaries (upper and lower control limit) on a control chart that help analyse the variation within a process.

Cp and Cpk indices (see Process capability indices)

Cross-functional process map
Cross-functional maps are often the preferred method of displaying process activities where more than one person or department is involved in the process. They also help identify process boundaries and process owners, and who is responsible for which activities or steps within a process.

Define-Measure-Analyse-Improve-Control (DMAIC)
This is the most commonly used process improvement methodology within Six Sigma, usually applied to existing processes.

Define-Measure-Analyse-Design-Verify (DMADV)
Six Sigma project steps, predominantly used to design a new product or service.

Design For Six Sigma (DFSS)
A specific version of Six Sigma mainly applied to design processes.

Deming Prize
This prize was established in 1951 in Japan as the world's first national quality award scheme to commemorate the contributions of the American quality guru Dr Edwards Deming to the development and application of statistical quality control techniques throughout Japan. The Deming Prize has several categories, including one category for individuals and one for overseas companies.

Discrete data
Discrete data are based on counts and can be put into classes. In contrast to continuous data, which can take on any value, discrete data can only take on discrete (fixed or exact) values. For instance, responses to a five-point scale questionnaire can only take on the values between 1 and 5, not values between whole numbers such as 2.53 or 3.75. Another example is the number of defective parts or invoices.

(The) European Model for Business Excellence (EFQM)
Founded by the Presidents of 14 major European companies in 1988, EFQM is the counterpart of the MBNQA (Baldrige Award) of the USA and Deming Prize of Japan, and is used to judge entrants to the European Quality Awards.

Executive champion (ExCH)
The highest role within a typical Six Sigma infrastructure, usually performed by the managing director or CEO of a company or business unit, the executive champion leads the Six Sigma initiative and makes high-level decisions during its deployment.

Failure-mode-and-effect-analysis (FMEA) chart
A graphical tool that is used to analyse

failure modes, their effects and root causes in order to identify actions for improvement

Gantt chart
A time plan that identifies the actions to be taken, their due dates and assigned personnel.

Green Belt
A competency-based Six Sigma qualification level. Green Belts, usually selected from the staff levels within a department, are an important part of Six Sigma as they are directly involved in the execution of the Six Sigma projects.

Histogram
The histogram, also referred to as (the) frequency plot(s), is a graphic display of classified or grouped data and their distribution frequencies.

Input-process-output (IPO) diagram
A commonly used graphic display of inputs and outputs of a process.

Malcolm Baldrige National Quality Award (MBNQA)
Established in 1987 in the USA and named after the Secretary of Commerce Malcolm Baldrige, the MBNQA is given to companies in five different industry sectors to recognize their quality improvement efforts.

Master Black Belt
The highest competency-based Six Sigma qualification level which is usually obtained by Black Belts after successful completion of a number of Six Sigma projects. Other qualification requirements (may) include abilities to teach other Six Sigma facilitators the Six Sigma methodologies, tools and applications and to act as consultant to all functions and levels of the organization, including the champions.

Matrix
A graphic display of the relationships between data sets organized in columns and rows.

Mean (*see* Average)

Metrics (Y)
'Metric' simply means measurement or using the metric system. In Six Sigma jargon the term 'metrics' is often used to describe the measurement of process outputs.

Outcome
The final result (effect) of an output on the (internal or external) customer.

Output
The amount of goods and work produced by a person, machine or process. Output can be in form of products, materials, services or information.

Pareto chart
A graphical display of bars by frequency and in descending order. Most Pareto charts have a second axis on the right-hand side with the cumulative percentage of each bar allowing the identification of the Pareto principle (80/20 rule).

Pareto principle (80/20 rule)
In general, 80 per cent of an outcome (effect) is obtained by 20 per cent of factors (causes). (This principle was first used by Vilfredo Pareto, an Italian economist, who found out that 80 per cent of the wealth was owned by 20 per cent of the people in the country.)

Precision
The resolution of a measurement. The higher the resolution, the more precise the measurement.

Process
A set of interrelated activities that transform inputs into outputs. A typical process has a start, an end and a purpose, and is linked to other processes.

Process approach

A method or concept that puts emphasis on defining, measuring, analysing and improving business processes in order to optimize organizational results. Process approach is the centre of Six Sigma.

Process capability

The ability of a process to produce satisfactory results.

Process capability indices *Cp* and *Cpk*

The ratios between the permissible spread (the specification tolerance) and the actual (natural) spread (three or six times sigma) of a process. Unlike *Cpk*, the process capability index *Cp* does not take into account the difference between the process centreline and the target (nominal) value.

Process flow (PF) chart

A graphic display of material or information flow within a process. It illustrates the steps and activities of a workflow from start to finish in sequential order.

Process map

A graphic representation of a process or an entire operation. Two most commonly used methods include the process flow chart and the cross-functional process map.

Quality Circle (QC)

Group of people often tasked with solving quality problems in their own work area.

Quality Function Deployment (QFD)

A practical and commonly used tool that helps translating customer requirements into design or process requirements. It can also be used to evaluate and prioritize a number of items by using a set of selection criteria.

Reliability

A tangible quality characteristic of a product or service for its functional performance.

Repeatability

Variation in a series of measurements that have been obtained by one (same) person with one (same) measurement device from one (same) measurement item.

Reproducibility

Variation in average measurements that have been obtained by two or more persons with one (same) measurement device from one (same) measurement item.

Run chart

A graphical display of a data set (individual observations or grouped data) over a specified period of time that helps identify trends or patterns.

Sample

A portion of the whole collection of items (population) that is taken in order to study the characteristics of the population.

Sigma

The nineteenth letter of the Greek alphabet. Sigma in lower case (σ) is used to donate standard deviation of a population. The capital letter (Σ) is the symbol for sum of a data set.

Sigma (σ) levels

If used as a measure of performance of a process, each sigma level (one sigma, two sigma, and so on) corresponds with a certain amount of defects. Sigma levels can also be used to compare output from different processes.

Six Sigma

A robust quality and process improvement concept that is built upon a well-defined infrastructure involving staff from several organizational levels in the so-called Six Sigma projects to drive the company's continual improvement efforts. As a metric, 6 σ (six times sigma) refers to 3.4 defects per million opportunities.

Special cause (of variation)

Reason for or source of failure that is not part of the whole system or inherent in the process itself. Its occurrence is intermittent, non-periodic, non-random or not predictable.

Specification (tolerance) limits

Technical values of a quality characteristic of a product (or service) which define the minimum requirements (boundaries) on its performance. Specification limits, sometimes referred to as the engineering tolerances, are usually set by customers, management or engineering department.

Standard deviation

A statistical measure of the variation or spread within a data set that is usually calculated from the squares of the deviations of the measures from the average. It is typically used as a measure of performance of a process.

Statistical process control (SPC)

Simply put, SPC is a concept or methodology that propagates the application of statistical tools and techniques to control processes. The term 'statistically controlled process' describes the condition of a process which after removal of all special causes (of variation) exhibits only variation with random or predictable pattern (common causes).

Total quality management (TQM)

A management approach that puts an emphasis on the continuous improvement of business processes through participation of employees from all levels of the organization in the so-called quality improvement teams or quality circles (QC).

Trivial Many (Xs)

Factors that are believed to have a positive or negative impact on a result.

Vital Fews (Critical Xs)

Borrowed from the Pareto principle, the term 'Vital Fews' indicates that only a few of the many factors have a significant (negative or positive) impact on the result.

Voice of the business (VOB)

The summary of all business needs or requirements including resources, organizational structures, technology, market trends and competition.

Voice of the customer (VOC)

The summary of all customer needs or requirements including expressed and assumed needs and requirements.

Voice of the process (VOP)

The summary of all process needs or requirements including materials, machines, people, information, methods, physical and non-physical environment.

Index

Hasan Akpolat, PhD

Senior Lecturer, Faculty of Engineering, University of Technology, Sydney
Director, RES-Q Management Services Pty Ltd

Hasan Akpolat holds a Bachelor of Engineering in Metallurgy, a Master of Engineering in Materials Engineering, and PhD in Materials Science from the Technical University Berlin, Germany. He is currently a Senior Lecturer in the Faculty of Engineering at the University of Technology, Sydney, where he coordinates and lectures subjects in Master of Engineering Management, the Faculty's core postgraduate programme taught in Australia and Asia. In 2003, Hasan headed the 'Management, Policy and Practice' Group, one of the four departments within the Faculty of Engineering.

Dr Akpolat's current research interests and consultancy practice include quality and operations management both in manufacturing and non-manufacturing industries with a particular emphasis on process analysis and improvement, risk management in operations and supply chain management.

Dr Akpolat has more than 16 years' of industrial experience in both manufacturing and service operations which spans over three continents. He has managed operations and production processes in industries as varied as mining, printing, packaging, medical devices, telecommunications, electronics, and electrical engineering, wholesale and retail sectors.

Hasan held several senior management positions with leading multi-national companies including Siemens, Johnson & Johnson, and Sony, involving strategic planning, change management, Total Quality Improvement and Six Sigma programmes that have delivered significant productivity improvement and cost reduction outcomes. From 2000 to 2002, he was the certified Master Black Belt responsible for the implementation of Six Sigma at Sony Australia and New Zealand.

Dr Akpolat is a widely recognized speaker and chairman of national and international conferences on quality and operations management including Six Sigma and process management and improvement. Hasan is also the founding Director of RES-Q Management Services Pty Ltd, a company specialized in high-level consultancy and training in quality and process improvement.

He can be reached at: hasan.akpolat@uts.edu.au
Website: http://www.eng.uts.edu.au/~hasan